Planning and Managing
AppleTalk® Networks

D1603725

Addison-Wesley Publishing Company, Inc.

Reading, Massachusetts ▪ New York ▪ Don Mills, Ontario

Wokingham, England ▪ Amsterdam ▪ Bonn ▪ Sydney

Singapore ▪ Tokyo ▪ Bogotá ▪ Santiago ▪ San Juan

Apple Computer, Inc.

© Apple Computer, Inc., 1991
20525 Mariani Avenue
Cupertino, CA 95014-6299
(408) 996-1010

Apple, the Apple logo, AppleLink, APDA, AppleShare, AppleTalk, Apple IIGS, A/UX, EtherTalk, ImageWriter, Inter•Poll, LaserWriter, LocalTalk, Macintosh, MacTCP, MultiFinder, ProDOS, and TokenTalk are registered trademarks, and Finder is a trademark, of Apple Computer, Inc. Classic is a registered trademark, licensed to Apple Computer, Inc. HyperCard and MacDraw are registered trademarks of Apple Computer, Inc., licensed to Claris Corp.

Adobe Illustrator and PostScript are registered trademarks of Adobe Systems, Inc. AlisaShare is a trademark of Alisa Systems, Inc. cc:Mail is a trademark of cc:Mail, Inc. CompuServe is a registered service mark of CompuServe, Inc. DECnet, PATHWORKS, VAX, VAXshare, and VMS are trademarks of Digital Equipment Corp. EtherGate, NetModem, NetSerial, and TeleBridge are trademarks of Shiva Corp. EtherPrint is a trademark of Dayna Communications, Inc. 4th Dimension is a registered trademark of ACIUS/ACI. GraceLAN and Technology Works are trademarks of Technology Works, Inc. IBM and OS/2 are registered trademarks of International Business Machines Corp. InBox is a trademark of Sitka Corp. LANSTAR is a registered trademark of Northern Telecom. Lotus is a registered trademark of Lotus Development Corp. MACLAN Connect is a trademark of Miramar Systems, Inc. Microsoft and MS-DOS are registered trademarks, and Windows is a trademark, of Microsoft Corp. NetWare is a registered trademark of Novell, Inc. NuBus is a trademark of Texas Instruments. PacerShare is a registered trademark of Pacer Software, Inc. PhoneNET and TrafficWatch are registered trademarks, and Liaison, NetAtlas, StarController, and Timbuktu are trademarks, of Farallon Computing, Inc. PhotoLink is a registered trademark of Photonics Corp. QuickMail is a trademark of CE Software, Inc. Retrospect Remote is trademark of Dantz Development Corp. StarGROUP is a registered trademark of AT&T. Sun is a trademark of Sun Microsystems, Inc. 3COM is a registered trademark of 3COM Corp. UNIX is a registered trademark of UNIX Systems Laboratories.

Simultaneously published in the United States and Canada.

ISBN 0-201-52345-0
ABCDEFGH-DO-91
First printing, AUGUST 1991

Publication Team

Writer: Sondra Garcia

Editor: Steve Rudman

Art Director: Joyce Zavarro

Production Editor: Debbie McDaniel

Designer: Lisa Mirski

Project Managers: Patrick Ames and John Gorham

Key technical contributors: Rich Andrews, Bill Berner, Craig Brenner, Dana Harrison, Gary Henry, Dan Iliff, Alan Oppenheimer, Priscilla Oppenheimer, Scott Petry, Scott Rohlfing, Dan Torres, Robert Wohnoutka

Contents

Part 2 Planning Your Network / 25

Part 3   Managing Your Network / 165

10   Network Maintenance Guidelines / 167

Foreword

The Information Age is a revolution. It's a revolution that's global in scope, with few safe harbors for isolationists. It's a revolution in which winning organizations will be those that give individuals the chance to personally make a difference. It's a revolution in which our key challenge is — how do we maximize the human use of information?

At Apple, we've always been concerned about maximizing human potential. In fact, our vision as a company is to create products that empower individuals to do their best, and to provide tools that help them manage and control information. Part of this vision involves giving people access to other people and information beyond their desktop. In this regard, Apple's products, including Macintosh® and AppleTalk®, have brought new levels of functionality and usability to individuals as well as to workgroups.

Once regarded as little more than the hard-wired connection between a Macintosh and a LaserWriter®, AppleTalk has grown into a highly functional network system. There are more than three million nodes installed. AppleTalk works. It's very easy to use. It's very easy to install. And it's media-independent.

With AppleTalk, Apple has extended the reach of Macintosh users, whether they work in small groups or large organizations. As you read through this book and learn about administering an AppleTalk network, you'll see how easy it is to integrate the Macintosh into any networking environment.

Apple is actively extending the reach of Macintosh to enterprise-wide environments—environments that encompass an entire organization. To be successful, we must provide excellent integration into an increasingly multivendor world. That's why Apple has been such a strong supporter of the development of open systems.

Connecting is only part of the solution. The real value to our customers is in interoperability and distributed computing—that is, the ability to run applications and share data across a network as easily as if it were on your own desktop Macintosh.

This is a powerful concept that allows you to put the power you need most of the time on your desktop, while giving you easy access to higher-performance computers when you need it. This strategy means we can combine the ease of use of the Macintosh with very cost-effective higher performance computing across the entire enterprise.

Apple began with the revolutionary idea of "one person, one computer." A book like this underscores the fact that the future of personal computing involves more than just placing a computer on every desktop. Just as Apple Computer helped raise the standards for stand-alone personal computing with the Macintosh, we now want to raise the expectations for the connected personal computer with innovative "interpersonal computing" products. As one example, Macintosh File Sharing, which is built into Macintosh system software, makes it easier than ever before to share information with other people.

We need individuals to have powerful new kinds of tools that will help them work, think, communicate, and learn in new and exciting ways. As we continue to expand our vision of personal computing to include interpersonal computing, I hope the message is very clear that at Apple we never intend to take our focus off of the individual. That's where the dream began—and that's where the vision becomes a reality.

John Sculley
Chairman and Chief Executive Officer
Apple Computer, Inc.

Planning and Managing
AppleTalk Networks

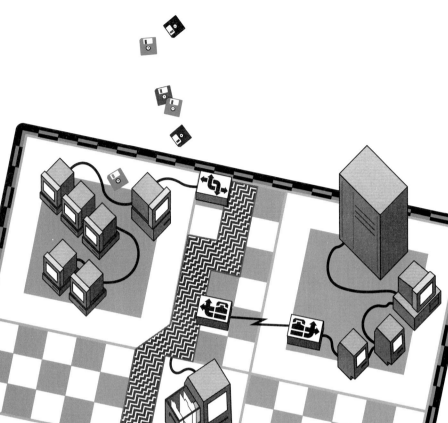
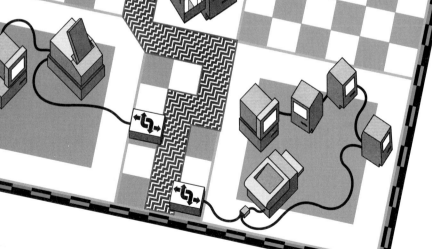

Part 1 Overview

The first part of this book—Chapters 1 and 2—contains an overview of the following topics:

- network administration, including a discussion of the administrator's role
- the book's intent and audience
- the book's organization and how to use the book
- basic concepts about the AppleTalk® network system, including a discussion of network protocols, the physical components of the network, and network addressing

If you are unfamiliar with network administration or with the AppleTalk network system, you will probably want to read some or all of the next two chapters. If these topics are already familiar to you, you may just want to read about the book's organization in Chapter 1 and then skip directly to Part 2, "Planning Your Network."

1 Introduction

When the first Macintosh® computer was introduced in 1984, it included an innovative capability in computer technology—built-in AppleTalk networking—that extended the Macintosh user's reach beyond the confines of the desktop. The initial AppleTalk networks consisted of three products—the Macintosh computer, the LaserWriter® printer, and LocalTalk® cables—that delivered shared printing service to users. Since then, the scope of the AppleTalk network system has broadened considerably. AppleTalk now supports other important industry standards, including Ethernet and Token Ring, and includes a variety of computers, peripheral devices, network services, and products, from Apple® as well as from other companies. Currently, the AppleTalk network system is used by more than three million computers in networks that range from a minimum of two devices to large internets with thousands of devices.

As the scope of the AppleTalk system has expanded, so have the responsibilities of those who administer these systems. Today, the network administrator's role is multifaceted, including such tasks as planning the network design, laying out cable systems, assessing and purchasing network products, day-to-day managing, and troubleshooting.

An administrator's job may encompass one of these areas or several, depending on the individual's level of experience and the size of the organization. In a large organization, the administrator may be responsible for administering just one of many networks in a larger, company-wide **internet.** Others in the organization may make network purchasing decisions, take care of cable installation, and handle network problems on the larger scale. In a smaller organization, the administrator may take on more of the planning and purchasing tasks, provide input to those who have these responsibilities, or be responsible for coordinating work (such as cable layout) with network contractors.

This book is written primarily as a guide for those who administer AppleTalk networks, although many other audiences, including business managers and network users, will also find the information valuable. The book focuses on small- to medium-sized networks, which can range from a single network to a small internet made up of several connected networks. It examines in detail the role of the network administrator, provides a solid background of AppleTalk network concepts, discusses the different kinds of services available for AppleTalk networks, and outlines the basic principles necessary to plan and manage an AppleTalk network effectively.

This book is *not* a review of the wide variety of products currently available for the AppleTalk network system, although the general types of products available and some specific examples are discussed. Because of the fast-paced nature of the computer industry, new products are introduced continually and, therefore, any reviews included here would be quickly out of date. Useful reviews can be found in a number of trade journals and magazines and are referenced in the Appendix.

Before reading this book, you should have a general understanding of local area networks and some knowledge about the computers you'll be using on your AppleTalk network. A number of introductory books on networking are available, including *Understanding Computer Networks* from Apple Computer (available at your local bookstore). You do not need to have any previous knowledge of AppleTalk networks or experience as a network administrator.

Who is the network administrator?

The administrator plays a central role in the design, operation, and maintenance of a network. Being a good network administrator is more of a learned art than an exact science and, as many administrators will attest, experience is usually the best teacher. However, there are certain qualities that go a long way toward ensuring success in this position, as discussed in the following list.

- *Technically inclined.* Although the person chosen to act as an administrator does not need to be an engineer or programmer, he or she is often required to troubleshoot both hardware and software problems. In addition, administrators must be willing to learn about computers in detail, because users will call upon administrators frequently to answer questions and to provide information.

- *Enjoys learning about applications and network-related subjects.* The administrator is a central source of information and should, therefore, be a generalist, familiar with all computers and applications used on the network—even applications that are *not* network related. When the administrator doesn't know the answer, he or she should be able to direct people to other sources that can help.

- *Enjoys the challenge and reward of investigative problem-solving.* Some responsibilities of the administrator involve a certain amount of detective work, such as alleviating network bottlenecks or discovering the source of network breaks, and are best carried out by a person who likes piecing clues together to solve a problem.

- *Trusted and respected.* Because administrators have complete control over the network—including access to confidential information—they must have a high degree of honesty and integrity.

- *Able to spend sufficient time maintaining the network.* Small networks require little time to administer. However, as networks grow and become more complex, they require more time to maintain and troubleshoot.

- *A clear sense of organization and attention to detail.* Especially when troubleshooting, the administrator must know where to look for clues. In addition, the administrator must be able to think through and formulate operational policies and procedures for the network and communicate them clearly to users.

- *Enjoys working with people.* Administrators must interact with a wide variety of personalities on a day-to-day basis. They must maintain a sense of balance and remain calm, even when under pressure.

Very often, administrators in small- to medium-sized networks simply "slip" into the role—either because they are told that this is now part of their jobs or because they are the only ones in their group who have the technical interest or skill. Administration is often just part of their regular job, whether that job is as an accountant, advertising executive, or word processor.

As an administrator, you may find yourself in charge of the only network in the organization. Or you may be responsible for a network that is part of a larger, company-wide internet. In either situation, your responsibilities will fall into some or all of the following categories:

Planning

This is the research phase during which you determine what your network needs are. You'll assess what kinds of network services you need, such as printing, file sharing, and electronic mail. You'll select the type of transmission medium to use and decide which network type (such as LocalTalk or Ethernet) is best suited to your requirements, based on such factors as network activity and numbers of users. You'll also evaluate different network products, design the network layout, and consider various factors that might affect your network installation. In addition, you'll take a look at security issues and determine what, if any, impact they will have on your network.

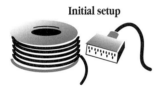

Initial setup

During this phase, you'll lay out the cable or help coordinate the installation with a professional installer, connect devices to the network cables, and install the appropriate software on computers and servers. You'll then check to make sure that everything is working as it should, and you'll teach people how to use the network.

Network maintenance

Maintenance consists primarily of routine tasks that keep the network running smoothly. You'll keep network logbooks; periodically monitor network activity using reports and software tools; add or relocate users and shared devices; back up and restore data; upgrade system software; train new users; manage your network servers; and analyze and alleviate any bottlenecks that occur.

Troubleshooting

Whenever users have problems working on the network, you'll spend time diagnosing and fixing problems. The amount of time you spend troubleshooting depends on the complexity of your network, the sophistication and experience level of your users, and your own experience as an administrator.

As you can see, administration covers a wide range of tasks. Your job may encompass just one or two of these areas, such as day-to-day maintenance of servers and basic troubleshooting, or it may involve all of these areas to some degree.

What's the best way to use this book?

There's no "right" way to use this book. Even though each chapter does build upon the previous one, you can also go directly to a subject that interests you rather than read the book sequentially. Additionally, if you are already familiar with certain basic networking topics (such as transmission media or topologies) or with the fundamentals of the AppleTalk network system, you can skip those chapters entirely.

The book is organized into three parts. Part 1, "Overview," lays the groundwork for the rest of the book, discussing basic terms and concepts relevant to network administration and to the AppleTalk network system. Chapter 1 (this chapter) has provided an overview of AppleTalk network administration. Chapter 2 provides you with an overview of the AppleTalk network system itself, covering such topics as network **protocols** (the rules that govern how the network system functions), the physical components of networks, and network addressing.

Part 2, "Planning Your Network," covers the various issues you need to consider as you design your network. Chapter 3 looks at the network services for AppleTalk, including printing, file sharing, modem sharing, and electronic mail, and helps you evaluate which services you might need. Chapter 4 discusses the different kinds of **media** that can be used on AppleTalk networks, from phone wire to infrared connections that eliminate the need for cable. Chapter 5 examines the ways in which you can physically arrange devices and weighs the pros and cons of each. Chapter 6 covers different network types, such as LocalTalk, Ethernet, and Token Ring, that target the needs of different network environments. Chapter 7 guides you in the design process, answering such questions as where to locate printers and servers and when it makes sense to create two or more connected networks. Chapter 8 looks at the various factors that can affect network installation, such as building and fire codes and electrical considerations. Chapter 9 helps you define your needs for network security and explores your security options.

Part 3, "Managing Your Network," discusses the ways in which you can keep your network running efficiently once it is set up. Chapter 10 provides guidelines for monitoring and maintaining your network, including information on backing up shared files, managing servers, supporting and training users, and optimizing network performance. Chapter 11 discusses network troubleshooting, providing information on administrative tools and strategies that can help you resolve problems, common situations you may run across, and some real-life troubleshooting scenarios.

The Appendix points you to additional sources of information on AppleTalk networks, network products, and local area networks. It includes a list of relevant publications from Apple with a brief description of each. It also includes other sources of networking information, such as computer journals, user groups, electronic forums, and networking books (both general and AppleTalk-specific). Terms of special significance to administrators are **boldfaced** throughout the book and are defined in the Glossary.

2 The AppleTalk Network System

The AppleTalk network system makes possible such activities as sharing information, sharing printers and modems, and communicating with others. An AppleTalk network consists of network hardware—such as computers, peripheral devices, and connection components—and network software, which runs in each device connected to the network.

This chapter provides an overview of the AppleTalk network system by discussing

- the AppleTalk protocol architecture, which governs how the hardware and software work together

- physical components, such as computers and connection hardware, that can be used on an AppleTalk network

- the addressing scheme, which describes how information is sent to the correct device

- the different types of networks, such as LocalTalk and Ethernet, over which AppleTalk protocols can operate

What is the AppleTalk network system?

The AppleTalk network system can best be described in terms of its *protocol architecture* and its *components*. The **protocol architecture** governs how the network's components communicate with one another. The **components** are all of the network's functional parts. This includes the hardware—such as computers, shared printers, servers, transmission media, and connection devices—and the software, such as network control software and network services. The following sections discuss these two aspects of the AppleTalk network system.

The AppleTalk protocol architecture

AppleTalk's protocol architecture determines how the various components on the network—devices, connectivity components (such as cables and connectors), and software—work together to provide network services to users. **Protocols** are the *rules* for exchanging information on the network and distinguish one type of network system from another. For instance, AppleTalk networks use different protocols than those used by TCP/IP networks, the network system most often used to connect UNIX® workstations.

Protocols govern nearly everything a computer network does by defining the actual steps that a device or program must take to communicate with another device or program on the network. The protocols define—among many other things—how devices can exchange information, how information is addressed or sent to the correct destination, and how multiple devices can send information on the same medium in an orderly way.

As a simple analogy of what protocols do, consider the various "rules of the road" that regulate how vehicles move from one place to another. The protocols that govern this process determine everything from what side of the road we drive on, to who has the right-of-way, to when we can proceed and when we must stop. We've all experienced the chaos that results when these driving protocols are not followed! Similarly, network communication protocols also define a process—the process of sending and receiving information over the network from one device to another. These protocols are very precise and must be followed by all network devices to interact successfully with each other on the network.

Protocols govern nearly everything a
network does, including...

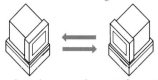

...how devices exchange information

*...how information is addressed and
sent to the correct destination*

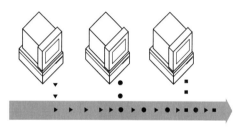

*...how multiple devices can send information
on the same medium in an orderly fashion*

Network protocols can be divided into three general categories:

■ *Application protocols* are the highest-level protocols. They enable an application
program to communicate with an equivalent application on another computer.

■ *Delivery protocols* are middle-level protocols. They manage the addressing scheme
that defines how information gets to and from a device on a network.

■ *Connection protocols* are the lowest-level protocols. These govern the physical
transmission that provides a path for information to travel from one device to another
on the network **medium,** such as cable.

As shown in the following figure, each time an interaction takes place between devices—for example, when a user requests a print job from a printer—data moves through each of these protocol categories in order to implement the request.

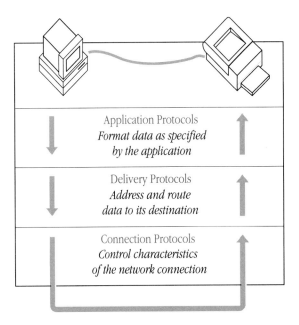

Application Protocols
Format data as specified by the application

Delivery Protocols
Address and route data to its destination

Connection Protocols
Control characteristics of the network connection

Protocols can be further divided into *layers* that describe the specific functions they govern. The International Standards Organization (ISO) has developed a reference model for layered network protocols that has become widely used to describe network protocol architectures. This model is called the **Open Systems Interconnection (OSI) model.**

A network is said to use protocols, or observe protocols, but protocols aren't physically tangible parts of the network.

One common source of confusion is that people sometimes talk about protocols "doing" a network task or "controlling" some aspect of communication. This implies that protocols are active entities on a network— which they are not. When you read, for example, that some networking protocol "manages interactions between computers and printers," this means that the protocol was written to *specify* how those devices communicate. The protocol itself is not a thing that resides on the network and manages other things on the network. Protocol rules are *adhered to* by networking software and by devices each time they perform a task, such as transmitting a document from one computer to another.

The OSI protocol model

In some ways, the OSI model is like a company organizational chart. Just as the organizational chart defines who performs what functions in the company, the OSI model defines which protocol layer is "in charge" of which functions in a network environment. The OSI model divides network protocols into seven interconnecting layers—physical, data link, network, transport, session, presentation, and application— that communicate with each other in a specified manner. The model starts at the lowest layer by defining the rules characterizing communication on the physical media, and continues through the highest layer, where services specific to user applications are provided. Each layer provides a defined set of services for the layer above and requests specific services from the layer below. Table 2-1 shows how the AppleTalk protocol architecture can be placed into the framework of the OSI model.

The AppleTalk protocol architecture is an **open system architecture,** which means that the protocols are openly published so that developers can implement them on other computer platforms. For more information on the AppleTalk protocol architecture, refer to *Inside AppleTalk,* second edition, and the *AppleTalk Network System Overview,* both listed in the Appendix.

Table 2-1 AppleTalk and the OSI model

	OSI reference model	AppleTalk protocols	Function
Application protocols	Application	Application-specific protocols that control such applications as AppleShare®	Provides the network services required by user applications.
	Presentation	AppleTalk Filing Protocol (AFP), PostScript	Prepares the information for the application, converting data formats as necessary for network transmission.
Delivery protocols	Session	AppleTalk Session Protocol (ASP), Printer Access Protocol (PAP), AppleTalk Data Stream Protocol (ADSP), Zone Information Protocol (ZIP)	Establishes a session and manages the sequence of interaction between two communicating devices.
	Transport	AppleTalk Transaction Protocol (ATP), AppleTalk Echo Protocol (AEP), Name Binding Protocol (NBP), Routing Table Maintenance Protocol (RTMP)	Controls the continuity and reliability of a communication transmission between devices; converts names to addresses.
	Network	Datagram Delivery Protocol (DDP)	Manages communication between multiple AppleTalk networks, addressing and routing data to its final destination in the internet.
Connection protocols	Data Link	LocalTalk Link Access Protocol (LLAP), EtherTalk Link Access Protocol (ELAP), TokenTalk Link Access Protocol (TLAP)	Times and coordinates the transmission; controls access to the network medium.
	Physical	Specifications that govern the network hardware	Defines the electrical and mechanical characteristics of the network connection and the media.

Network components

Whereas the protocol architecture provides a *conceptual* view of how the system functions, a discussion of the network components focuses on the network from a *physical* perspective, examining the tangible pieces that can be used on the network. There are three basic components on an AppleTalk network:

- computing and peripheral devices
- connection hardware
- networking software

The following sections provide an overview for each of these components. In some cases, you are referred to later chapters in the book that discuss a subject in more detail.

Computing and peripheral devices

By using the AppleTalk network system, you can connect a variety of dissimilar computers and peripheral devices. Besides the Macintosh family of computers, many other personal computers can be part of an AppleTalk network, including the Apple IIe, Apple IIGS®, and MS-DOS computers.

Other types of computers, including the Digital VAX™, IBM mainframes, and computers running the UNIX operating system, can also communicate with AppleTalk devices through a variety of networking and communications products. For example, AppleTalk for VMS™ enables a VAX computer to act as a device on an AppleTalk network, making it possible for AppleTalk users to take advantage of the computer's processing power, file storage capacity, and wide area network resources. When using a Macintosh computer running the A/UX® operating system, AppleTalk allows Macintosh computers to communicate over Ethernet networks with computers running under the UNIX operating system, such as Sun workstations. There are several publications listed in the Appendix that provide more information on connecting to other computer environments, including *A Guide to Apple Networking and Communications Products, Apple Multivendor Network Solutions Guide,* and *Introduction to the Apple-Digital Network Environment.*

Additional computing devices on an AppleTalk network include **servers** that, when combined with special networking software, can provide network services such as file service, electronic mail, and print spooling to users on the network. Macintosh computers and other computers, such as the VAX and MS-DOS computers, can all be used as servers.

Shared peripheral devices are also common components of an AppleTalk network. These include modems, printers, plotters, and scanners, and can be a mixture of Apple and non-Apple products.

Connection hardware

AppleTalk connection hardware consists of

- the transmission medium and connectors

- transceivers

- devices called *repeaters, bridges, routers,* and *gateways*

The **transmission medium** and connectors link individual devices on the network. AppleTalk can operate over a variety of transmission media, including twisted-pair, coaxial, and fiber-optic cable as well as infrared light. These options enable you to select the medium that best fits your network requirements. (Refer to Chapter 4 for a discussion on evaluating transmission media.)

The **transceiver** is the hardware that transmits and receives information between a device and the network medium. The transceiver may be built into the computer or the peripheral device (as in the case of LocalTalk, discussed in Chapter 6). Alternatively, the transceiver may be added to each device through an external transceiver module, an interface card, or an external **SCSI** box.

When you need to go beyond the limitations of a single AppleTalk network—for instance, if you need to connect two separate networks or if you need to enlarge a network that has reached its maximum length of cable or number of devices—you can use **repeaters, bridges, routers,** and **gateways.** These devices are either dedicated hardware or special networking software that is installed in a computer. When two or more networks are connected together with a router, the resulting system is called an *internetwork,* or **internet.** The connected networks can be near one another or they can be geographically distant and connected through modems. (Chapter 7 provides a detailed discussion of internets and connection devices such as routers.)

Media *enable information to flow between devices.*

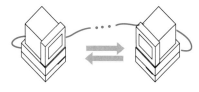

Transceivers *transmit and receive information between the device and cable.*

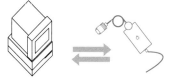

Repeaters, bridges, routers, and gateways *enlarge or connect networks.*

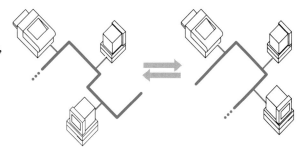

Networking software

You can use a variety of networking software on an AppleTalk network for such functions as

- implementing network connections
- providing network services
- performing network management and troubleshooting tasks
- performing bridging and routing
- providing networking applications

Network connection software, sometimes referred to as network **drivers,** control the network transceivers that send and receive information. Drivers enable devices on the network to transmit and receive data on the network medium and to communicate successfully with one another. The LocalTalk driver is included with the operating system of most Apple computers. The drivers for other network types (such as the EtherTalk® driver for Ethernet and the TokenTalk® driver for Token Ring) must be added to each device (see Chapter 6 for a discussion of Ethernet and Token Ring networks).

Another type of software is used for **network services,** which enable users to perform such tasks as sharing files, using a shared printer, and exchanging electronic mail. These services use software that runs on network servers and on each **client computer** using the service. The **AppleShare File Server** is an example of network service software that runs on a Macintosh computer, providing file-sharing service to users. Network services are the topic of Chapter 3.

Network management and troubleshooting software helps administrators monitor the network and diagnose the source of problems that arise. For example, the **Inter•Poll**® administrator's utility searches for and reports on all active devices connected to an AppleTalk network. Network management and troubleshooting are discussed in Chapters 10 and 11.

Routing and bridging software is installed on the computers or other hardware used to connect AppleTalk networks together. The **AppleTalk Internet Router** is an example of routing software that is installed on a Macintosh computer. (See Chapter 7 for a discussion of routers and bridges.)

Networking applications are the software tools used for such activities as setting up group calendars and sharing a central database. Network applications make possible a wholly new way for people to collaborate and work more productively. However, administrators also need to be aware of such network issues as software licensing agreements and whether applications can manage concurrent access by multiple users. These issues are explored in Chapter 10.

AppleTalk addressing

A network system must have some method to identify network devices so that the information being transmitted can be sent to its correct destination. That scheme is called **addressing.** Addressing is the fundamental method by which all networks manage the transfer of information. When network software performs a task, like sending a file to a printer or transmitting a mail message between users, the software requires the addresses of both the sender and recipient.

The AppleTalk network system uses an addressing scheme that identifies both the sender and recipient by means of *node* and *network numbers.* A **node** is any device that might be the target of a transmission on the network, such as a computer or a

LaserWriter printer. Each node's address contains a **node number** (or **node ID)** and, in an internet, also identifies the network to which the node is connected, called the **network number.**

The information that is transmitted between nodes is organized into **packets.** A packet includes

- the user information that is being transmitted

- the addresses of the sender and recipient devices

- additional information about the type or purpose of the transmission. This information tells the network device at the receiving end (and any connecting devices along the way) what to do with the packet.

AppleTalk packets vary in length from a few characters to several hundred. A short network transmission might fit into a single packet, while a longer transmission, such as a document file, will usually be broken up into multiple packets. Some of the packets transmitted on a network are not sent by users, but by network software implementing AppleTalk protocols, such as routing devices that exchange network information in order to update other routers.

By examining packet activity, you can gauge the amount of activity on your network as well as the integrity of network connections and transmissions. In Chapter 10, you'll learn how packet analysis can be used to monitor your network.

The AppleTalk network system uses node and network numbers to identify the sender and recipient. Information is sent between nodes in the form of packets.

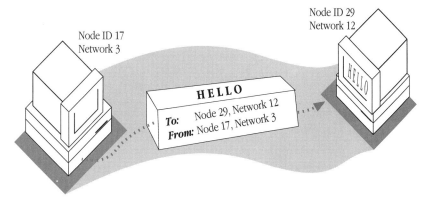

Node ID 17
Network 3

Node ID 29
Network 12

HELLO

To: Node 29, Network 12
From: Node 17, Network 3

Dynamic node assignment

Unlike network environments where nodes have fixed addresses, AppleTalk nodes automatically assign themselves a node address each time they start up. This scheme is known as **dynamic node ID assignment.**

In network environments where node addresses are fixed, the network administrator has extra hardware and software configuration to do. For example, the administrator may have to set the node address manually for each device, add each address to a central database so that other devices can communicate with the new device, and keep track of addresses for the devices in the organization.

Dynamic node assignment eliminates such typical network configuration procedures. Adding a device to an AppleTalk network is simply a matter of plugging in the device to the network cable (once any necessary interface cards are installed); the device is then up and running as a node on the network. Since addresses are not fixed, nodes can also be moved without concern for taking node numbers that are already in use.

A node may or may not have the same address each time it is turned on. When restarted, a node attempts to reclaim the address it previously used. If, while the node was off, its address was acquired by another node, the node will acquire a new address.

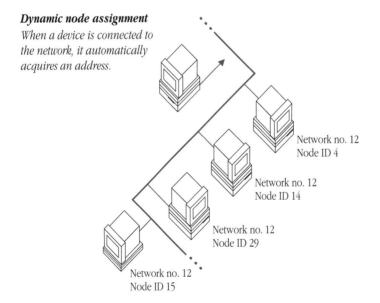

Dynamic node assignment

When a device is connected to the network, it automatically acquires an address.

Network no. 12
Node ID 4

Network no. 12
Node ID 14

Network no. 12
Node ID 29

Network no. 12
Node ID 15

AppleTalk's naming service

Although networks require numerical network addresses to identify devices, such as printers or users' computers, these addresses can be difficult for people to remember and use. Because of this, AppleTalk enables users to identify devices using meaningful *names* instead. AppleTalk network software automatically translates these names into network addresses by using AppleTalk's **Name Binding Protocol** (NBP).

When a device is connected to the network, NBP assigns a useful name (such as LaserWriter) to the device. Alternatively, administrators can name devices with names they choose. For example, the Namer application enables administrators to name print devices on the network.

Besides making it easier for users to refer to and access devices, "name binding" means that device names can stay the same even when devices move. This makes network modifications simpler, since you don't have to reconfigure each device to "tell" the network where the device is located.

Once a device is connected to the network and the appropriate software is installed on the device, it is immediately visible to all users, by name, through the **Chooser.** No additional hardware configuration is needed for users to access different devices. Users can simply browse through the Chooser to select the network device they need to use.

AppleTalk users can select devices using meaningful names.

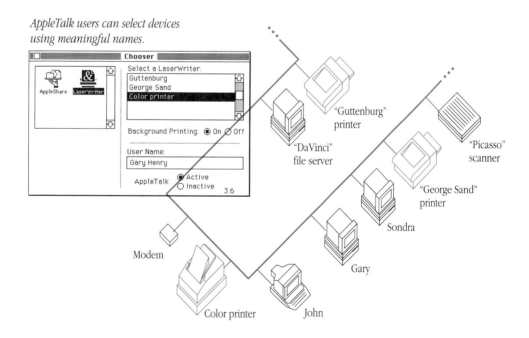

Network types

AppleTalk protocols can operate on several different kinds of networks, including **LocalTalk, Ethernet,** and **Token Ring.** These network types differ in many respects, most notably in terms of transmission speed, cost, the number of devices that can be connected, the distance that can be covered, and ease of installation. You can connect different network types together by using a router, enabling all computers to communicate with one another and to share devices such as printers and file servers. Regardless of the network type you choose, each provides the same AppleTalk services and ease of use throughout your internet.

LocalTalk is a low cost, easy-to-install network that is well suited to small work-groups with low to moderate amounts of network activity. The network connection for LocalTalk is built into all Macintosh computers and many peripheral devices, such as printers.

Ethernet is an industry-standard, high-performance network that is used to accommodate heavy amounts of network activity, cover longer distances, connect many devices, or provide very quick response times. Devices are typically connected to Ethernet networks by using EtherTalk software and an interface card.

Token Ring is an industry-standard network that is commonly used to connect IBM mainframes and IBM PCs. Macintosh computers can be connected to a Token Ring network by using TokenTalk software and an interface card.

You'll learn more about these network types in Chapter 6.

Conclusion

As you've learned in this chapter, the AppleTalk network system can be viewed in two ways: conceptual and physically. The conceptual point of view examines the network protocols that govern how the system functions. The physical point of view looks at the actual components that reside on the network, such as devices and connection hardware. This chapter has also provided an overview of addressing: how information is sent to the correct place, how a device automatically acquires a network address, and how AppleTalk's naming service translates names into network addresses. Finally, you've learned about the different network types—LocalTalk, Ethernet, and Token Ring—over which AppleTalk protocols can operate.

Because of AppleTalk's open system protocol architecture, you can expect new AppleTalk networking products and services to be introduced frequently—from both Apple and other companies. You can keep up with the latest products for AppleTalk networks in many ways: through computer magazines, user groups, trade shows, and electronic bulletin boards (see the list of references in the Appendix for some helpful reference sources).

With this broad overview of AppleTalk in mind, we now move on to the second part of the book, "Planning Your Network." Part 2 begins by introducing the variety of network services you can use on AppleTalk networks, such as print service, file service, and electronic mail. Subsequent chapters discuss such planning issues as choosing the right transmission medium, evaluating network topologies, designing your network, and network security.

Part 2 Planning Your Network

There are many issues to consider as you begin planning your network. Taking the time to think through and assess your network needs is an important step in designing a network that will meet tomorrow's needs as well as today's. The following are some key questions you should ask yourself:

- *How many users need to be connected?* This is one of the most important considerations in planning your network, since it determines the network's initial size. Do you have a few dozen users or a few hundred? How will this number change in the next year or so?

- *Where are users located and how much distance does the network need to cover?* Are users located on a single floor, multiple floors, or in more than one building? Are offices separated by movable partitions or are there solid floor-to-ceiling walls? What will the total network distance be? Are there any remote users who need to access the network?

- *What kinds of network services and application software do users need?* Do users need to share files; share printers, modems, or other peripheral devices; or exchange electronic mail? Do they need to share applications over the network?

- *What kind of network activity will these services and applications generate?* The kinds of applications and services being used and the number of people using them can affect network activity and design. For instance, if your network will have a great deal of activity on it, it might be a good idea to create two smaller, connected networks rather than a single large network.

- *What kinds of devices will be on the network?* Do you need to connect different types of computers, such as Macintosh, MS-DOS, VAX, and Apple II computers? What other devices will you need (shared printers, servers, modems, scanners, film recorders, and so on)? How many will you need? What special interface cards and software might you need to connect these devices to the network?

- *Which network type best fits the current and near-future physical, work-related, and budgetary requirements of your network?* Will LocalTalk be sufficient to meet your needs or will you need to use Ethernet to accommodate a large number of users or heavy network activity?

- *What kind of transmission medium best serves your network needs?* Factors such as existing wiring, cost, ease of installation, the size and layout of your site, and security can all affect your choice of media.

- *What are the physical considerations that can affect your installation?* How will your network be laid out? Where will cable be run? Does your site have special environmental requirements?

- *Which users need to communicate with one another?* Do different groups need to communicate or share resources? In what ways do they need to communicate? For instance, does the group you're responsible for need to exchange electronic mail with a department in another part of the building?

- *Do users need to access computers on other networks, such as DECnet or TCP/IP?* What special software or hardware might you need to connect to these large systems or other networks?

- *What level of security do you need on the network?* Is the data on your network highly confidential? Will you need to take strict precautions to guard against unauthorized access or accidental loss?

- *What are your plans for the future and how might they affect your network plans today?* Do you anticipate expansion in the coming year or two? Will you need to add many more people or additional floors to the network, or will you need to connect different computers to the network?

Chapters 3 through 9 will help you answer these questions and will guide you through the planning process.

3 Assessing Network Services

Network services deliver the benefits of networking to users, enabling them to work more efficiently and effectively—as individuals or as part of a team. These services make it possible for users to access and share information and applications, collaborate electronically, share network resources such as printers and modems, and communicate quickly with other people on the network.

This chapter explores the following network services and helps you evaluate which ones you might need on your network:

- print services
- file services
- electronic mail
- remote dial-in access to the network
- modem sharing

How are network services provided?

Most network services are provided by devices called *servers*. A server can consist of a dedicated piece of hardware, a central computer with specialized software, or even a user's personal computer that is set up to provide services to other people on the network.

AppleTalk networks commonly include many kinds of servers, including file servers, print servers, electronic mail servers, and modem servers. In the past, servers were often dedicated to providing just a single network service. Today, with a sufficient amount of memory and disk space, a single server can fulfill many roles, providing multiple services—such as print and file service—simultaneously.

Note that some network services, such as shared printing, can be provided without using a central server—an option that may be appropriate for smaller networks. However, servers provide certain features and efficiencies, such as centralized administration, that may be needed in larger networks.

AppleTalk print services

Print service is often the first network service that is set up on an AppleTalk network. In fact, the very first AppleTalk networks were LocalTalk networks that connected a few Macintosh computers to a shared LaserWriter printer. Because AppleTalk networks enable users to share printers, the printing cost per user is kept at a reasonable level. This is particularly advantageous when using applications such as those for desktop publishing, where very high-quality output and equally high-quality (and expensive) printers are required.

You can use a wide variety of printing devices on an AppleTalk network, both from Apple and from other companies. Printing can be set up in one of two ways: by using a shared printer or by using a *print server,* which takes over the printing task from users' computers. The following sections discuss the types of printing devices you can use on your network and the different methods you can choose to set up printing.

Using Apple printers

Apple's network printing devices are designed with the AppleTalk network system in mind. This means that printers can be easily attached directly to the network, either through a connection built into the device or by adding interface hardware to the device. It also means that computers include the printer *drivers*—the programs that tell a computer how to work with specific types of devices—as part of the system software. All Apple printers implement the AppleTalk Name Binding Protocol (NBP), which allows users to access devices by *name,* through the Chooser, rather than by a cumbersome address. Additionally, all Apple printers support the advanced graphics capabilities of the Macintosh computer.

There are currently two families of printers for AppleTalk networks: ImageWriter® and LaserWriter. ImageWriter printers are dot-matrix printers that can provide letter-quality shared printing. ImageWriters require a LocalTalk Option Card to connect to a LocalTalk network. These printers offer versatile paper-handling features that are especially useful for such tasks as printing labels, multipart forms, and letters. LaserWriter printers are laser printers that provide fast (up to eight pages per minute), near typeset-quality shared printing (300 dots per inch). LaserWriters for AppleTalk networks have built-in LocalTalk connections.

Using printing devices from other companies

You can also connect a variety of printing devices to an AppleTalk network that are sold by companies other than Apple, including high-resolution phototypesetting equipment, daisy-wheel printers, plotters, and line printers. These non-Apple devices may differ from Apple printers in several ways.

For one, the way these devices connect to the network varies considerably. Non-Apple devices can be connected to an AppleTalk network through a built-in connection; through an adapter; or through an intermediary device that is connected to the network.

Secondly, unlike an Apple printer in which the printer drivers are included with the system software, non-Apple printing devices may require you to install special drivers in order for the devices to work in your operating environment.

Another difference may lie in the way users select the device. NBP may or may not be an integral part of a non-Apple printing device, depending upon how the device was designed. If the printing device does not adhere to NBP, users may have to select the device through some means other than the Chooser.

Finally, some non-Apple printing devices may not support the high-resolution graphics capabilities of the Macintosh. For instance, printing devices such as high-speed line printers are intended for text applications rather than graphics.

Shared printing

One way to set up network printing is by simply connecting an appropriate printer to the network cable, making the printer available to everyone on the network. When users send documents directly to a shared printer, they have to wait for their print jobs and all print jobs ahead of theirs to finish before their computers are free for other work.

Shared printing is well suited to small networks or to networks where users print at different times. However, if the printing workload is heavy and many users need to print at the same time, shared printing can result in bottlenecks and subsequent loss of productivity while people wait to regain control of their computers.

Shared printing
*Users wait for their print jobs
and all print jobs ahead of theirs to finish
before their computers are free.*

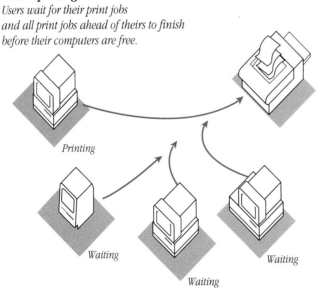

Printing

Waiting

Waiting

Waiting

With shared printing, you can also use **background printing,** which allows a user to continue working on other tasks while his or her document is being printed. The background printing software runs on a user's computer as a **background process.** When a user issues a print command, the background printing software stores the document on the user's hard disk and then sends the document to the printer when the printer is free. The user's computer must remain connected to the network until the document is processed. If the computer is turned off, or if its connection to the network is broken, the print job will not be printed. Background printing may occasionally slow the performance of a computer until the document is actually sent to the printer.

Background printing
A user can continue working while his or her document is sent to the printer.

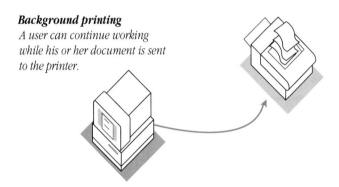

The **PrintMonitor** application program included with Macintosh system software is an example of a background printer. Aside from the speed and convenience provided by background printers, they also provide users with additional management control in printing their own documents. For example, with PrintMonitor users can

- see the name of the document that is currently being printed, the document's status (for example, how many pages still need to be printed), and the name of the printer being used

- see the names of their documents waiting to be printed and get general information about each document's status

- cancel a print request

- specify a date and time to print a document

- receive an alert notice if any printer problem occurs (for example, if the printer is out of paper)

- be immediately notified when a manual-feed job starts (for example, to print labels)

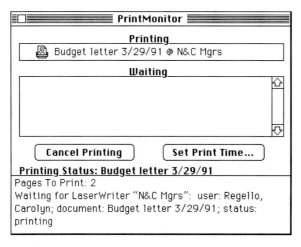

PrintMonitor lets users see the status of their documents.

Printing with a server

An alternative way to set up network printing is to use a **print server,** sometimes called a **spooler.** The server allows several users to send documents to the same printer simultaneously, regardless of whether or not that printer is currently busy. Rather than having to wait for the printer to become free, users transmit their files to the server and immediately regain complete control of their computers for other tasks.

A print server consists of special software operating on a computer with one or more hard disks. This server computer acts as an intermediary between one or more computers and one or more printers. When users issue print commands, their documents are sent (or *spooled*) to the server and are stored on the server's hard disk, completely freeing their computers of printing tasks. The server sends each document to the appropriate printer when the printer is available to print the user's document.

Print servers are effective for networks that use printers regularly. From a user's point of view, the process used to print with a server is no different than that for printing directly to a network printer. Users issue the same commands they would normally use to print to their usual print devices. However, users will definitely notice how quickly their computers are freed for other work.

Printing with a server
Many users can send documents
to the same print server and regain control
of their computers for other tasks.

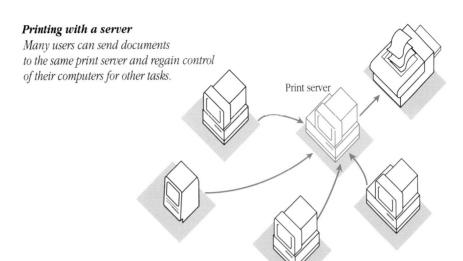

Print server

A print server is managed by the network administrator, providing a single point of control over print jobs and a variety of options to monitor printer usage.

The **AppleShare Print Server** can handle printing for up to five networked ImageWriter and LaserWriter printers, which can be located in different AppleTalk **zones.** It consists of server software that runs on a Macintosh computer and it can be used by Macintosh, Apple II, and MS-DOS users.

An AppleShare print server provides you with a variety of information to help you centrally manage and control printing for a group of users. For example, you can

- interrupt printing or spooling for printer or network maintenance
- defer printing
- immediately print a high-priority document
- delete a document in the queue
- view the current status of the print server and associated printers. You can see whether the server is connecting to a particular printer or if printing has stopped because a printer is out of paper. You can also view the status of each document in the print queue, the name of the user printing the document, the date and time the document was sent to the server, and the number of pages in the document.

- bypass the server to print directly to a network printer. This option is useful if, for example, you need to print using the manual-feed option on the printer.
- refer to an automatically generated print log about documents that have been printed, documents that were deleted from the print queue, and documents that could not be printed

Print Spooler Queue				
Status: PrinterError: no paper tray				

Status	Document	User	Date/Time	Pages
	15 –Appendix A /Special...	Wong, John	4/3/91 10:38:20 PM	8
	N & C Survey-Layer#1	James, Patricia	4/3/91 10:47:40 PM	1
	2/18/91CC	Berkeley, Ron	4/3/91 10:38:22 PM	1
	Speech draft	Garcia, Janet	4/3/91 10:44:46 PM	2
	16-Appendix B/Special K	Henry, Mark	4/3/91 10:47:44 PM	21

The AppleShare Print Server lets you display the status of the server, the printer, and each document in the print queue.

Background printing or print server: Which one to use?

How do you know whether to use background printing or a print server? If your network is small, background printing may be all you need. A server may not be economically feasible for your network. Or you may not need central control over print jobs and background printing may be adequate to speed up the printing process from the user's point of view.

As your network grows, however, and contention for printers increases, a print server is often most efficient. The server completely frees computers from the printing tasks so that users can get on with their work. A print server also allows you to centrally manage printing tasks for a group. In addition, a print server provides users with some handy features not provided by background printing, such as the ability to shut down their computers once documents are sent to be printed.

AppleTalk file services

AppleTalk file services provide users with a convenient and productive way to access and share information and applications. These services are provided by **file servers,** which are typically computers with specialized software and one or more attached hard disks or **CD-ROM** discs that store the shared information.

You can use a file server to do the following:

- access and use files and applications that reside on a server
- copy files and applications from a file server to your own computer
- store files and applications on the file server so that others can readily access them

You can share information on a file server in two ways: over time—you place a file there and others access it later—or simultaneously, where several people can access and update a file at the same time.

File servers can be big timesavers. It's certainly much easier and faster to place a file on a server instead of distributing multiple floppy disks, or to place a document in-progress on a server so that it can be viewed or annotated electronically by contributors rather than passing the document around from office to office.

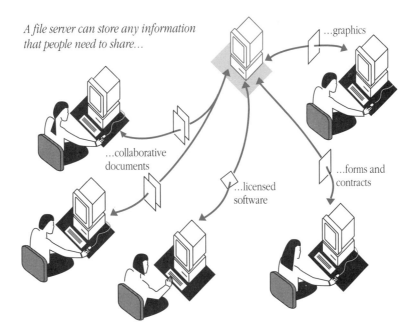

A file server can store any information that people need to share...

...graphics

...collaborative documents

...licensed software

...forms and contracts

AFP: Computer-to-server communication

Communication between a user's computer and a file server is made possible by the **AppleTalk Filing Protocol,** commonly referred to as **AFP.** AFP server software can reside on a variety of hardware platforms. Typically, these platforms are general-purpose computers, such as one of the Macintosh family of computers, MS-DOS computers, and the Digital VAX. However, some AFP file servers consist of dedicated hardware that is connected to an AppleTalk network. Regardless of the hardware platform used as an AFP file server, standard client software is used to access the server.

AFP provides users with a number of significant features:

- *Extension of native operating environment.* Files and application programs on the server are accessed and used as if they were located on the user's personal computer. For instance, when a Macintosh user logs on to a file server, the file server icon appears on the desktop just like any other attached disk. Macintosh users see the usual Macintosh interface with its familiar icons, choose icons by pointing and clicking, and copy files by dragging them to their local disks. Similarly, MS-DOS and Apple II users access and use the server in a way that is familiar to them.

- *Consistent server interface.* Whether the server platform is a Macintosh, an MS-DOS computer, or a Digital VAX, users access and use file service in a consistent fashion.

- *File security.* Access to the server is restricted by user names and passwords. Users can protect their individual folders through an access privilege scheme.

- *A shared, dynamic view of the file server.* Whenever anyone makes a change to the contents of the file server, that change appears on the computer of each user logged on to the server—regardless of whether the computers are dissimilar. For example, if someone creates a new folder, that folder will show up on each user's desktop with the appropriate access privileges assigned.

Note that file servers using filing protocols other than AFP can also be used on an AppleTalk network. However, file server applications in a non-AFP environment do not adhere to the features and standards discussed above and may be accessed differently and may use a different interface than AFP servers.

Centralized file service and distributed file sharing

AppleTalk file service can be centralized or distributed. **Centralized file service,** as its name implies, is provided by a central server that is accessed by users. The server does not usually run user applications, such as word-processing or spreadsheet programs, but it does often provide other network services, such as print spooling and electronic mail. A centralized server is managed by a network administrator who performs such duties as registering users, monitoring and controlling server usage, and backing up shared files.

Distributed file sharing can be provided by *any* personal computer on the network that has the file-sharing software installed. In effect, each user's computer becomes a file server, enabling users to share the contents of their hard disks with other users on the network. The file server software operates in the background of each user's computer and can be used concurrently with other applications. In such a distributed system, individual users are responsible for managing file service.

The decision to use centralized or distributed file service is based upon the needs of your organization. In general, distributed file sharing should be considered when you have a small group of users (less than ten) who need to share files. In this situation, distributed file service can be very cost effective, since you don't need to dedicate a computer to its use. In addition, if there's no need to centrally control file server usage or if you have little time to manage a file server, distributed file sharing may be a good choice. Note that the performance of a computer running file-sharing software will decline when the computer is being shared by others on the network.

Centralized file service is appropriate for groups of more than ten users. As the number of users increases, centralized service delivers better performance than distributed file sharing, because the central server is only performing the file server tasks rather than running other applications that typically exist on a user's personal computer. Centralized service also makes it easier for many users to locate the information they need. In addition, the ability to centrally manage file service becomes more important in larger groups, enabling administrators to monitor and control server usage from a single location.

Other considerations include backup and security. When you have many users, it's much easier to back up one central server rather than a multitude of servers. And centralized file service enables you to physically restrict access to the server by locking it in a secure room.

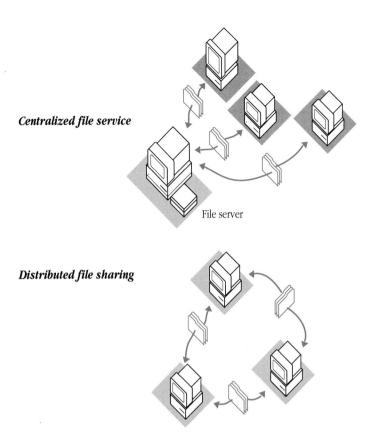

Centralized file service

File server

Distributed file sharing

The next two sections provide examples of centralized and distributed file services from Apple: the AppleShare File Server and Macintosh File Sharing.

The AppleShare File Server: Centralized file service

The **AppleShare File Server** is a central location where AppleTalk users can store and share information and applications. AppleShare consists of server and administrative software that runs on a Macintosh computer and computer-specific workstation software for Macintosh, Apple II, and MS-DOS computers.

Information is stored on an AppleShare file server on attached disks (either hard disks or CD-ROM discs) called **volumes.** Within a volume, files are stored in folders. These AppleShare folders are analogous to directories on a PC or a UNIX computer. Both folders and directories are named and they hold files or other folders/directories. AppleShare enables users to share entire volumes or specific folders within a volume.

AppleShare file service is equally well suited to small groups in one geographic area or to diverse user populations scattered throughout a large internet. A single server can accommodate over a thousand users, with 50 users connected at any one time. A single network or internet can include many file servers, and with the right access privileges, any user can access any connected server.

Registering users and creating groups

Some organizations prefer that information be completely accessible to all users, and they do not require file protection schemes. If this is the case for your organization, you can use AppleShare by simply setting up the appropriate hardware and software and having users log on as **guests.** However, because many organizations prefer to keep certain information private, AppleShare provides data protection for these networks. You can specify which users can access a server volume and who can create folders by first registering users on the server with a name and a password. You can then assign specific privileges to those users.

Registering users on an AppleShare file server

You can also organize users into one or more **groups** to reflect the way they'll share information. (A user can belong to many AppleShare groups.) Groups can be organized by any criteria desired, such as department, project, or location. You can assign the group to a particular folder and assign special access rights to the group. For example, a project team may want you to set up a group of users with whom they can share confidential information, making the information inaccessible to others on the network.

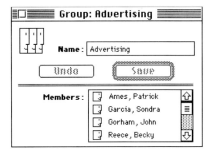

Specifying an AppleShare group

Using the server

Users access an AppleShare file server by first selecting it from the Chooser. They are then asked to enter their names and passwords, as shown in the following figure. If you have not registered users, they can log on as guests (if you make the file server available to guests). As users enter their passwords, the characters show up as dots or asterisks so that no one can see the password as it is being entered. AppleShare passwords are also **encrypted** as they are sent over the network to eliminate the possibility of electronic eavesdropping. (Note that AFP file service from other companies may not encrypt passwords.)

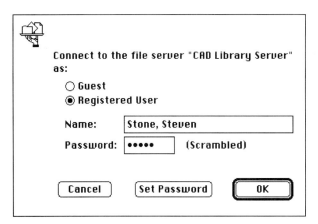

Logging on to an AppleShare file server

After users log on to a file server, they can select the volumes they want to use. Each selected volume appears on their desktops and users can then display the contents of each volume. On the Macintosh screen, the AppleShare folders, files, and volumes appear in the form of icons. Macintosh users can open files and folders by double-clicking with the mouse. On an MS-DOS computer, AppleShare folders appear as directories and sub-directories; documents appear as files. MS-DOS users can use standard DOS commands to open files and folders. The following screens show a view from a Macintosh computer and an MS-DOS computer logged on to the same AppleShare file server.

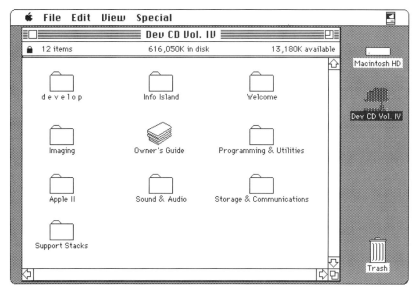

A view from a Macintosh computer logged on to an AppleShare file server

```
C:\WORD>dir d:

 Volume in drive D is !DEU_CD_UOL
 Directory of   D:\

!APPLE_I I   <DIR>      06-25-90   11:30p
!D_E_U_E L   <DIR>      03-06-90    1:42p
IMAGING      <DIR>      03-06-90    3:54p
!INFO_IS LAN <DIR>      03-06-90    1:41p
!OWNER'S GU      350816 07-05-90    6:37p
!PROGRAM MIN <DIR>
!SOUND_& AU  <DIR>
!STORAGE &   <DIR>
!SUPPORT ST  <DIR>      06-15-90   11:14a
WELCOME      <DIR>      07-02-90    1:30p
        10 File(s)   13496320 bytes free

C:\WORD>
```

A view from an MS-DOS computer logged on to an AppleShare file server

File security

AppleShare protects files in two ways: through password security and through access privileges to specific server volumes and folders. Administrators can set access privileges for *any* folders stored on the file server. Individual users can set privileges for the folders *they* create. When a registered user creates a folder on the file server, that user is the owner of the folder. The owner decides who can access each folder and what kind of access other people can have (such as reading or making changes to the information). Guests cannot create private folders and can only access public folders, which are available to everyone who can access the server.

AppleShare access privileges at work

Here's an example of how AppleShare's access privileges might be used. (Note that Don is using AppleShare in the System 7 environment.) Don is collaborating on a publications research report with Paul and Gail. Don asks you to set up a group on the server, called *Focus Group*, and to include Paul, Gail, and himself in this group. Don then creates a folder on the server called *Focus Group Results*. Using the User/Group category, he specifies See Folders, See Files, and Make Changes privileges for the Focus Group team so that they can all add their comments to the report. When he finishes the first draft of the report, he places it in the group folder.

Later, Don decides that it would be a good idea to let the rest of his Publications department read the report in progress, but doesn't want anyone else in the department to make changes to it. So, using the User/Group category once again, he specifies that his Publications group (which you've already created) has See Folders and See Files privileges. He doesn't specify any access privileges for Everyone, so other people with access to the server will not be able to read the report.

User/Group:	Focus Group	Publications	Everyone
Folder icon:	Focus Group Results	Focus Group Results	
Access privileges:	See Folders See Files Make Changes	See Folders See Files	None

---

With AppleShare, administrators and users can specify three kinds of access privileges that can be used in combination with one another.

- *See Folders* allows others to see the folders (if any) nested within a volume or folder. If someone does not have See Folders privileges, the folders within the main folder will not appear on that person's screen.

- *See Files* allows others to see the files within a volume or folder and to open and copy those files onto their local disks. If someone does not have See Files privileges, the files within the main folder will not appear on that person's screen.

- *Make Changes* allows others to make changes to a folder, including moving, renaming, or deleting any of its contents, as well as adding files or folders.

These privileges can be granted to any of three categories of network users:

- *Owner.* Either the creator of the folder or any registered user or user group to whom the creator assigns ownership. This category allows the owner to restrict his or her own privileges; for example, not allowing accidental deletion of a file.

- *User/Group.* A single user or a specified group of registered users.

- *Everyone.* Every user with access to the file server, including guests.

The access privileges set in AppleShare are visually apparent to everyone using the server. Folder icons graphically reflect the kinds of access privileges that have been assigned, letting users know what kind of access (if any) they have to the information.

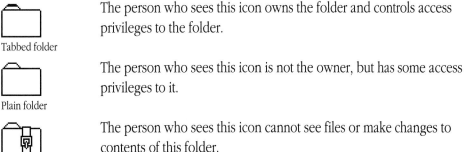

Tabbed folder — The person who sees this icon owns the folder and controls access privileges to the folder.

Plain folder — The person who sees this icon is not the owner, but has some access privileges to it.

Not accessible — The person who sees this icon cannot see files or make changes to contents of this folder.

Drop folder — The person who sees this icon cannot open the folder but can copy files and folders into it. This is often called a *drop folder* (or *drop box*). Once a document is placed into the drop folder, only the intended recipient (the owner) can retrieve and open it.

AppleShare management features

AppleShare provides several ways to control and track file server usage and performance:

- *Monitoring and controlling server usage.* You can view current server activity; copy-protect files; and lock files and folders so they cannot be renamed, discarded, or changed.

- *Displaying server status messages.* When you start up the server, you see status messages, such as the date and times of startup and the number of connected disks found. These messages are automatically recorded in a file server log and can help diagnose problems that arise.

- *Creating detailed administrative reports.* You can create AppleShare reports that provide information about the server and volumes (such as the amount of disk space used); existing files and folders; folder hierarchy and access privileges; and owner, group, and user names. Chapter 10 discusses how to use administrative reports to manage your network.

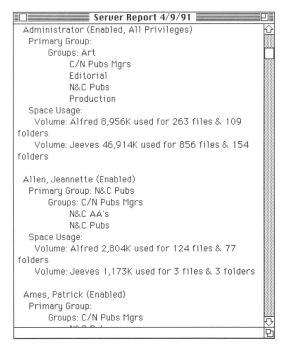

AppleShare reports provide a variety of information, including the amount of shared disk space used by each person and the groups to which each person belongs.

Macintosh File Sharing: Distributed file sharing

Macintosh File Sharing—a built-in feature of System 7—enables users to share information on their Macintosh computers with other people on the network. Any user whose Macintosh computer is running System 7 and has the file-sharing feature turned on can share files directly with other network users.

At all times, Macintosh owners have complete control over what information they share and with whom they choose to share it. For example, they can

- share the files in a folder with one other person
- share several folders with everyone on the network
- share an entire hard disk with everyone in their department
- keep the contents of their computers private and not share anything at all

Turning on File Sharing

Before files can be shared, computer owners must turn on File Sharing, as shown in the following figure. Once this feature is turned on, it stays on until it's turned off again.

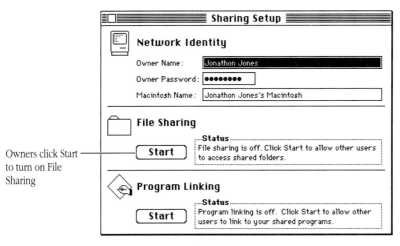

Owners click Start to turn on File Sharing

Turning on Macintosh File Sharing

The owner then selects specific folders and disks to be shared, specifying who can access them and what kinds of access privileges they can have. Access privileges range from the permission to view and copy information to the ability to make changes, store information on the owner's disk, and even create new folders and files.

A convenient feature of Macintosh File Sharing is that it allows Macintosh owners to access the entire contents of their hard disks from *any* computer on the network. This is very handy if, for example, you're in someone else's office and you need to check a file on your own computer.

Using File Sharing

Users can access other Macintosh computers in the same way they access a centralized file server such as the AppleShare File Server—through the Chooser. As shown in the following figure, the Chooser displays a list of all the servers available on the network, including the other Macintosh computers that have File Sharing turned on.

Once users are connected to another Macintosh computer, they can access shared folders and disks and create new documents if they have the appropriate access privileges to do so.

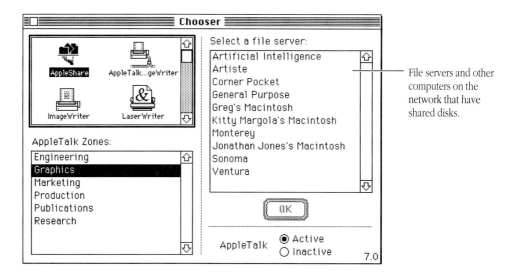

File servers and other computers on the network that have shared disks.

Monitoring File Sharing

Macintosh File Sharing includes a number of features for monitoring and controlling computer usage. Computer owners can readily gauge the file-sharing activity of their computers, displaying all of the folders and disks they are sharing and a list of the people currently connected to their computers (shown in the following figure).

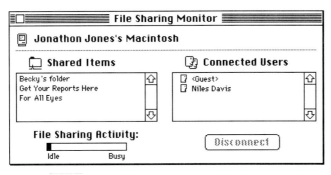

Macintosh File Sharing allows users to monitor file-sharing activity on their computers.

AFP file servers from other companies

Other companies have implemented AFP file service on hardware platforms other than the Macintosh. These currently include NetWare (from Novell), which typically runs on Intel-based computers; VAXshare™ (part of PATHWORKS™ for Macintosh, jointly developed by Apple and Digital Equipment Corp.), AlisaShare (from Alisa Systems), and PacerShare (from Pacer Software), all of which run on the Digital VAX; StarGROUP LAN Manager Server (from AT&T), which runs on UNIX-based computers; MACLAN Connect (from Miramar Systems), which runs on MS-DOS computers; as well as dedicated server platforms, available from a variety of companies. As shown in the following figure, users select other AFP servers through the Chooser in exactly the same way they select shared disks made available through the AppleShare File Server or Macintosh File Sharing.

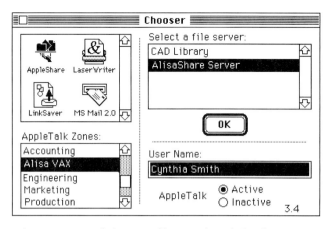

Selecting a non-AppleShare AFP file server through the Chooser

There are several reasons you may opt to use a non-AppleShare AFP file server. It might make sense economically if you already have that particular hardware platform (such as an MS-DOS computer). Or, you might need a particular connectivity solution that's solved by another AFP server; for instance, maybe you need to exchange files with users on a VAX. In addition, you might want to take advantage of some of the added features provided by the server, such as enhanced security or increased file storage capacity.

Novell's NetWare is one of the leading network operating systems for connecting MS-DOS computers. By installing Novell's NetWare for Macintosh software on a Novell server, Macintosh computers and other personal computers running MS-DOS, OS/2, and Windows 3.0 can all access the server's file-sharing and printing services. The server can be connected to a LocalTalk, Ethernet, or Token Ring network.

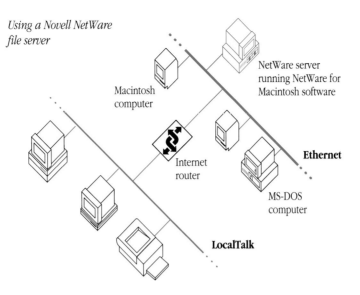

Using a Novell NetWare file server

NetWare server running NetWare for Macintosh software

Macintosh computer

Internet router

Ethernet

MS-DOS computer

LocalTalk

A Digital VAX computer can be used as an AFP file server and print server through such products as VAXshare, PacerShare, and AlisaShare. This means that Macintosh, MS-DOS, Apple II, and VAX users can share the same files as well as printers located on either a DECnet™ or an AppleTalk network. Computers on an AppleTalk network use the standard AppleShare client software to access the VAX server.

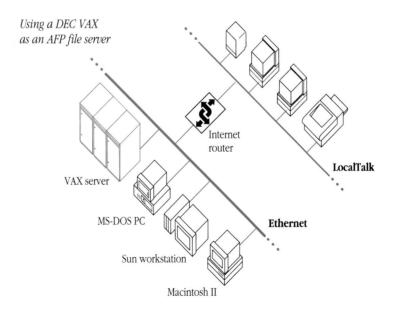

Using a DEC VAX as an AFP file server

Internet router

LocalTalk

VAX server

MS-DOS PC

Ethernet

Sun workstation

Macintosh II

The VAX file system appears on a Macintosh as a series of hierarchical file system volumes, with VAX directories being represented as folders and VAX files represented as documents. MS-DOS users can access VMS directories as MS-DOS directories. No translation process is necessary to move between the VMS and Macintosh or MS-DOS file systems. Users on Macintosh, Apple II, and MS-DOS computers can also access the VMS Distributed File Service to use files on other Digital systems connected to the VAX file server.

Using a VAX as a file server provides AppleTalk users with access to the large-scale computing power of the VAX, while retaining the look and feel of their usual working environments. This means, for example, that a Macintosh user can use the standard Macintosh desktop interface to access VMS files, such as quarterly financial figures, and then bring that data to the Macintosh for graphing. Or artwork can be prepared on a Macintosh and then printed on a typesetter that's connected to the DECnet network. By using a VAX as a file server, AppleTalk users also benefit from increased storage capacity. While acting as an AFP file server, a VAX conforms to standard VMS file system security.

Sharing files among different computers

AppleTalk file services enable Macintosh, Apple II, and MS-DOS computers to share files stored on a file server. In order to read a file on one computer that has been created in a different operating environment (for example, MS-DOS to Macintosh or Apple II to Macintosh), the files must have a common file format or else a **file translator** must be used.

Some applications have built-in file translators and do not require users to take any additional steps to read a file created in a different operating environment. For example, Lotus 1-2-3 files created on an MS-DOS computer can be stored on an AppleShare file server and then opened by a Macintosh user running Microsoft Excel.

Applications that do not have built-in file translators require a separate file translation program. The **Apple File Exchange** utility is one such translation program and is included with every Macintosh computer. Apple File Exchange comes with a set of translators for specific applications; you can purchase additional translators for Apple File Exchange if you need them.

Using electronic mail

Electronic mail, or **E-mail,** is a quick, convenient way for AppleTalk users to exchange text, sound, graphics, and binary data with other people in their organization. E-mail eliminates the time delays associated with "telephone tag" or regular postal delivery, enabling users to transmit information almost instantaneously—anyplace, anytime. It can be used across AppleTalk zones and network types (that is, LocalTalk, Ethernet, and Token Ring), linking people together in all parts of an internet system within an organization. Using modems, electronic mail can also link users that are geographically dispersed.

Users can create an electronic mail message or file within an E-mail application. Alternatively, they can send files that have been created using another application, such as their favorite word-processing or spreadsheet software. To send mail, users usually only need to know the recipients' names; the mail system can be set up so that users don't have to know where the recipients reside on the network.

Is a server needed?

An E-mail system can be designed to work with or without a central **mail server,** which is typically a computer with one or more hard disks for storing accumulated messages and files. In a serverless—or **direct delivery**—system, messages are sent directly from one computer to another. This requires that the computer receiving the mail be turned on when the message is sent. Direct delivery systems are useful in small networks where it may be impractical to have a server.

If the mail system uses a server, then that server acts as a **store-and-forward device.** The server is the intermediary between sending and receiving devices: it accepts messages, stores them in a user's **electronic mailbox,** and then sends the messages on to their destinations when requested by the recipients. In a server-based system, a user can send mail even when the recipient's computer is not turned on. To read their mail, recipients can log on to the E-mail system at their convenience, any time of the day or night.

Mail servers also provide additional features not offered in a direct delivery system. For instance, the server may provide centralized administration (making such tasks as backup easier) and a directory service that can be used to find the E-mail names of network users.

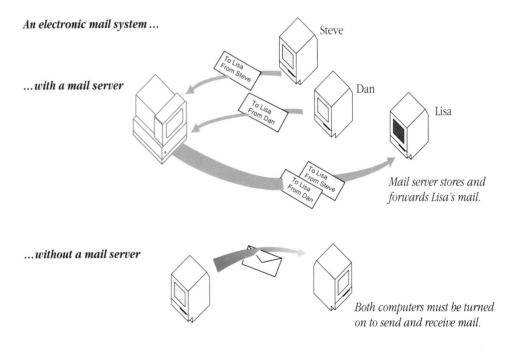

An electronic mail system ...

...with a mail server

Steve

Dan

Lisa

To Lisa From Steve

To Lisa From Dan

To Lisa From Steve
To Lisa From Dan

Mail server stores and forwards Lisa's mail.

...without a mail server

Both computers must be turned on to send and receive mail.

Mail servers need not be dedicated to mail service; they can also run concurrently with other network services such as print spooling or file sharing.

E-mail features

Ideally, it's best to have one E-mail system that everyone in the group can feel comfortable using. The system should be straightforward enough for novices and yet have enough advanced potential for sophisticated users.

E-mail software varies from vendor to vendor, but some of the more desirable features are listed below:

- audio and video alert messages that let users know immediately when a message has arrived
- address lists that enable users to specify individual recipients
- distribution lists that enable users to specify a group of recipients
- file enclosures or annotations that enable users to attach spreadsheets, graphics, sound, or text to a message
- automatic processing of mail, such as forwarding to a specific address
- an interface to applications so that an application can send mail directly
- the ability to sort messages, such as by date or name
- phone messages that can be sent electronically with all the standard phone message information
- password protection that can be changed by each user
- an easy way to save messages that users want to keep
- gateways, which enable users to read from and send to mail systems on other networks

Some products enable different computers on the network to exchange electronic mail (such as Macintosh and MS-DOS computers); others do not provide this capability. Some of the most commonly used E-mail packages for AppleTalk networks include Microsoft Mail, cc:Mail (cc:Mail), QuickMail (CE Software), and InBox (Sitka). For more information on these and other E-mail packages, refer to the trade journals and books about Macintosh networking listed in the Appendix.

Dialing in to your network

Will any of your users need to access the network while they're away from the office—for instance, if they're traveling on business or working at home? If so, you'll want to consider setting up a remote **dial-in service** on your network.

A variety of products enable users to connect their computers to an AppleTalk network from a remote location using a **modem** and ordinary dial-up telephone lines, including Liaison (from Farallon Computing), NetModem, TeleBridge, and EtherGate (all from Shiva Corporation). The remote computer can be on another network or not on any network. Once the remote computer is connected to the network, users can do anything they could do if they were connected locally to the network. For example, users can print a document on the office LaserWriter, send an electronic mail message to a coworker, or access files that reside on an AppleShare file server.

Products that provide remote dial-in access to an AppleTalk network can be hardware- or software-based. Hardware-based products are dedicated "black box" devices that sit between a user's computer and the modem. Software-based products consist of remote-access software that runs on a user's computer. Depending upon how the product is implemented, the access may be *one way* or *two way,* as shown in the illustrations on the following page. If access is one way, then only the remote end is able to access the devices on the network that is being dialed into. The network to which the remote device is connecting cannot access devices or services on the remote end. If access is two way, then the product functions as a **half-bridge** or **half-router** (described in Chapter 7). Users can access devices on either side of the half-bridge or half-router by selecting them through the Chooser.

Because remote access can potentially be an easy way for unauthorized users to access data on a network, most remote-access products provide some kind of security protection. Users are commonly required to identify themselves by name and password before they can access the network. Some products limit the number of unsuccessful call-in attempts, at which point the user's account is automatically disabled. A **callback** procedure is an additional security precaution in which the caller's preauthorized phone number is verified before allowing the user to connect to the network. A data encryption scheme may also be used in which a secret code scrambles the information being sent and makes it readable only by computers using the same code. Some products also enable you to restrict access to specific zones within a network.

One-way remote dial-in access

Through remote-access hardware or software
users can dial in to a network.

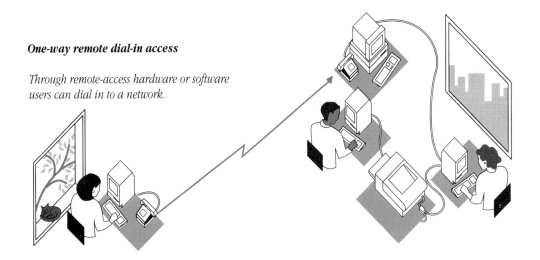

Two-way remote dial-in access

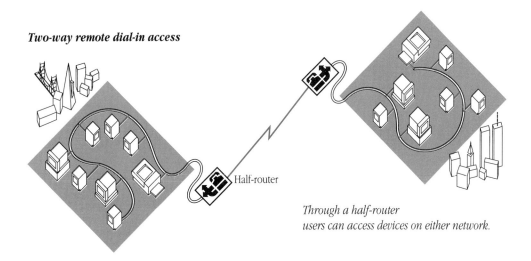

Half-router

Through a half-router
users can access devices on either network.

Sharing modems

If several users on your network need to use a modem, consider using a **modem server,** which eliminates the cost of multiple modems and extra phone lines. A modem server can be used to dial *into* the network from a remote location (using a remote dial-in access product) or to dial *out* of the network to access remote resources, such as on-line information services.

You connect a modem server directly to an AppleTalk network, and users select it through the Chooser. The server controls user access, allowing just one person at a time to use the modem, and letting users know when the modem is busy.

Some modem server products are software-based. The server software runs in the background on a Macintosh computer, and the client software runs on each computer that needs to access the server. Software-based products work with ordinary modems. Other modem servers consist of specialized hardware platforms and software that is installed on each client computer.

Two commonly used modem server products for AppleTalk networks are NetModem and NetSerial (Shiva Corporation).

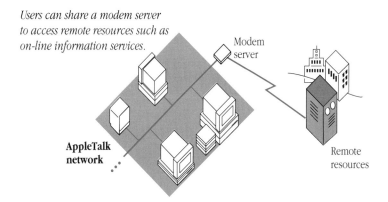

Users can share a modem server to access remote resources such as on-line information services.

Modem server

AppleTalk network

Remote resources

Conclusion

At this point, you probably have a good idea about what kinds of services you can use on your network. The next step is talking to users to find out what their exact needs are. Will they need to collaborate on projects electronically? Do many users need to perform on-line research outside the company, making a modem server a high priority? Will users benefit from a print server or will printing be very occasional?

Keep in mind that, if you need to, you can start out with just the essential services users need *today* and then add more services later on down the road. As your network expands, you'll probably need to expand your existing services (by adding more servers, for example) and add services that meet your users' new and changing needs.

If your administrative role is a part-time one, you may want to consider using services that place more of the responsibilities on the user rather than on you. For instance, distributed file sharing—controlled by each user—will be less time-consuming for you than centralized file service, where you are in charge of maintaining and managing the server. On the other hand, if your network is growing rapidly, you may benefit from many of the management and control advantages provided by centralized servers.

A final note: this chapter has focused on helping you evaluate which network services you need. Chapter 7, "Design Guidelines," will discuss server requirements in greater detail, providing guidelines on the amount of shared disk space and server memory you need as well as guidelines for running multiple services on one server.

4 Selecting the Right Medium

The **transmission medium** is the "thread" that links together computers and other devices, enabling them to communicate and share information. AppleTalk network types can use a variety of media. For example, the LocalTalk network type can operate over traditional cable methods—including shielded and unshielded twisted-pair cable—or it can send data by means of infrared light, a more recent development in network technology. This chapter explores the basic principles of media technology and helps you evaluate which medium best fits your network environment.

Some factors to consider

Given the variety of media available, how do you decide *which* medium to use? There are some clear-cut and important distinctions between different types of media that will help make your choice easier. Some of the factors to keep in mind include:

- **Network activity**

  What kind of transmission speed will you need to accommodate the activity on your network? Generally speaking, the greater the amount of network activity, the higher the transmission speed you may need. While a network's transmission speed is largely governed by the design of the network and the method of transmission, the media over which signals travel may also affect the maximum transmission speed. The physical properties of different media determine how suitable the media are for high rates of data transmission. Typically, the term **bandwidth** is used to indicate how much data can travel over the network media in a given period of time—the higher the bandwidth, the higher the media's capacity for transmitting data. (See Chapter 7 for a detailed discussion of network activity.)

- **The size and layout of your site**

  How much distance does the medium need to cover to connect all network devices and where are devices located? Because of attenuation—the weakening of electrical signals over distance—different types of media have a prescribed maximum length between devices as well as an overall maximum network length. (These lengths can be increased in a number of ways by using devices such as repeaters that extend the recommended cable length or by using routers or bridges to connect networks together, as described in Chapter 7.) Twisted-pair cable, for example, is generally used for short or moderate distances, while coaxial and fiber-optic cable are capable of transmitting data over longer distances.

- **Electromagnetic interference considerations**

  Does your network reside in an area of high interference? Radio transmitters, power transformers, electric motors, gasoline engines, and industrial machinery all produce **electromagnetic interference** (EMI), which can seriously affect the reliable transmission of network data. If your site generates a large amount of EMI, you may need to install fiber-optic cable or use infrared light, both of which are highly resistant to EMI.

- **Ease of installation and maintenance**

  Can you install and maintain the cable yourself? Depending on your level of experience, you might be able to plan the cable layout and install the cable yourself or you may have to rely on a more experienced person or a professional installer. Any changes that are made to the network, such as additions or reconfigurations, may also need to be handled by a professional installer. Some media, such as twisted-pair cable and thin coaxial cable, can generally be installed and maintained with relative ease, while other media, such as fiber-optic cable, require more technical expertise.

- **Cost considerations**

  How much can you spend? What are your budgetary constraints? Even though you may want fiber-optic cable, will you have the budget to support it? When considering cost, remember to include not only the purchase price, but the installation and maintenance costs as well. Twisted-pair cable is your least expensive option.

- **Security considerations**

  What are your security requirements? How sensitive is the information on your network? Some kinds of media are more susceptible to data monitoring and interception, either through electronic eavesdropping or cable tapping. If security is a critical concern at your site and you believe that your network is vulnerable to intrusion, fiber-optic cable may be your best choice.

- **Existing wiring**

  Does cable already exist in the building you occupy? In some cases, you may be able to take advantage of preexisting cable. Make sure, however, that the cable suits the requirements of your current—and near-future—network environment.

The following sections discuss your media choices, elaborating on the factors mentioned above, and will help guide you through the decision-making process.

The changing face of media technology

Although the descriptions in this chapter accurately reflect the current state of media technology, this technology is undergoing rapid advancements, blurring some of the boundaries and distinctions between media types. For example, although twisted-pair cable has traditionally been considered a low-speed transmission medium, ideally suited for low to moderate network activity, techniques have been developed to use twisted-pair for high-speed Ethernet transmission. Similarly, although fiber-optic cable is now considered difficult to install and an expensive desktop-to-desktop solution, the next generation of fiber-optic cable may make it an economically feasible alternative to twisted-pair and coaxial cable.

Twisted-pair cable

Twisted-pair cable consists of two wires, often made of copper, that are individually insulated and then twisted together. *Unshielded,* twisted-pair cable—the kind used in standard telephone systems—has insulation covering each of the wires, but there is no shielding between the wires and the outer insulation jacket. This lack of shielding makes the cable more vulnerable to electromagnetic interference from the environment it passes through. Another kind of twisted-pair cable is *shielded,* as shown in the following figure. Shielded twisted-pair (such as LocalTalk cable from Apple Computer) has an extra layer of shielding to provide some added protection from interference.

Shielded, twisted-pair cable

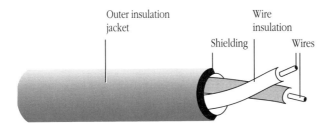

Twisted-pair cable is very popular because it is low cost, generally easy to install, and easy to reconfigure. The cable is very flexible and is commonly strung along baseboards, around corners, and under desks from computer to computer within the network. It is ideal for networks that carry a low to moderate amount of traffic and that span relatively short distances within a single building.

Twisted-pair does have some drawbacks, however. Because it lacks heavy-duty shielding, twisted-pair is not well suited to networks located near industrial operations. The cable should not be routed near electric motors, gasoline engines, welding machines, or any device that has a strong electromagnetic field, such as a power transformer or radio transmitter. If security is a major consideration, twisted-pair cable may not be a good choice, because signals can be radiated by the wires and intercepted electronically (unless the cable is enclosed in a special conduit). In addition, the physical ruggedness of twisted-pair is fairly low. It can be damaged in many ways, including improper installation, sharp bends, heavy objects resting on it, or people stepping on it.

Coaxial cable

Coaxial cable consists of an inner conducting wire and an outer surrounding ground wire (see the figure below). Between the conductor and ground is an insulating layer, and the entire cable is shielded. Although coaxial cable is more expensive than twisted-pair, its wider bandwidth permits faster transmission speeds and its extra shielding provides good protection in environments where twisted-pair could not function. It is particularly resistant to interference from sources such as radio transmitters. Coaxial cable provides improved security over twisted-pair because signals are not radiated by the wires. However, it is still easily tapped by anyone who can gain physical access to the cable.

Coaxial cable

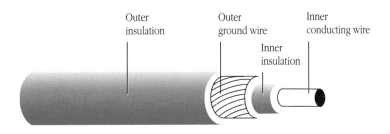

Outer insulation

Outer ground wire

Inner conducting wire

Inner insulation

There are two types of coaxial cable (also known as *coax*) commonly used in computer networks: thick (or *thicknet)* and thin (or *thinnet).* Thick coaxial cable measures about 1/2 inch in diameter and can extend almost two miles without substantial signal degradation. Because of its thickness and rigidity, thick coaxial cable is cumbersome to install. It is usually laid above a dropped ceiling, in a wire conduit, or beneath a raised floor, connected to individual computers through a **transceiver cable** (see the following figure).

Thicknet

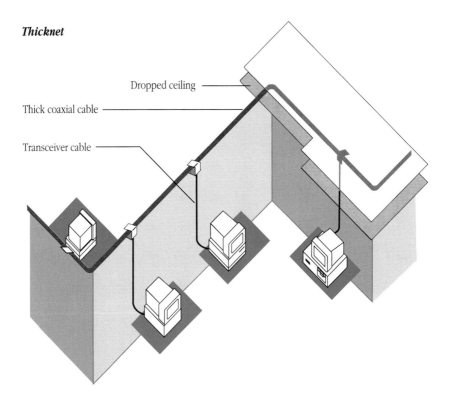

Dropped ceiling

Thick coaxial cable

Transceiver cable

Thin coaxial cable, which measures about 3/16 inch in diameter, is much like the cable used for cable TV. The distance it can span is less than thick coaxial, but it is less expensive and more flexible, making it easier to install. Thin coaxial cable snakes from computer to computer within the network. The cable is connected to each computer with a T-connector, as shown in the following figure.

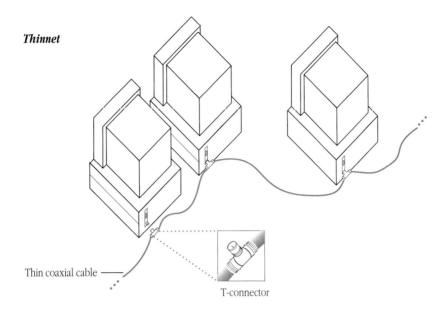

Thinnet

Thin coaxial cable ——

T-connector

Because the cable television industry has popularized the use of coaxial cable, there are many contractors who specialize in designing, installing, and maintaining coaxial systems, and there is a ready supply of standardized hardware for installation.

Fiber-optic cable

Fiber-optic cable uses light rather than an electrical current to send a signal through fine fibers made of glass (see the following figure). It can transmit signals at a very high speed over long distances, with a high degree of immunity to interference. The cable is rugged, has a long life, and is very reliable under adverse physical conditions.

Fiber-optic cable

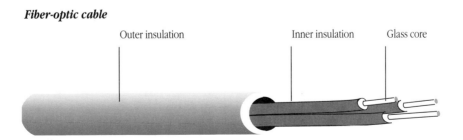

Outer insulation   Inner insulation   Glass core

Fiber-optic cable is ideal in installations susceptible to interference, such as industrial sites. It is also useful in high-security sites. For one, information is transmitted optically, rather than electronically, eliminating interception risks. For another, the cable is extremely difficult to tap. The cable's ruggedness, immunity to interference, and its ability to transmit data over long distances without signal degradation also make it useful for connecting buildings within an organization.

Installation of fiber-optic cable can be difficult (and therefore, expensive) and requires the use of special connectors and alignment techniques. In addition, there is currently a lack of standardization in the industry and a limited choice in companies that specialize in fiber-optic installations.

At the present time, fiber-optic cable can be an expensive desktop-to-desktop solution and is not well suited to small networks unless interference or security is a critical consideration. However, costs are dropping rapidly and developments in low-cost fiber-optic systems will probably make these networks commonplace in the future.

Infrared media

Infrared light, which is basically the same technology as that used to send remote-control signals to a TV set, provides a way to transmit data without using physical cables. In an open office, each network device is connected to a transceiver device that communicates with other transceivers by means of infrared signals bounced off the ceiling or wall. To network devices, these signals look just like those received by network cables. Infrared light can also be used between buildings by transmitting the signal through panes of glass.

Because installation of infrared networks involves simple installation of transceiver devices, these networks can be well suited to very dynamic environments where people are frequently moving from one office to another or where offices are often rearranged. Like fiber-optic technology, infrared light is immune to electromagnetic interference, so it is useful in environments that generate large amounts of interference, such as industrial sites. Infrared signals can be tapped by anyone within "line of sight" of the transmission, so it may not be appropriate for high-security requirements. As a relative newcomer to local area networks, infrared connection is not widely available at the present time. However, as this technology becomes more prevalent, the number of vendors offering it will most certainly grow.

Infrared light

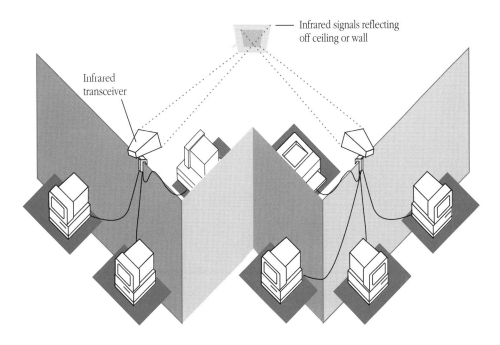

Infrared signals reflecting
off ceiling or wall

Infrared
transceiver

Conclusion

The array of media types may seem a little bewildering at first glance—how do you
decide which one is best? Choosing the appropriate transmission medium for your
network, however, can be relatively straightforward and is determined by your specific
network requirements in several well-defined areas, summarized in the following table.
Currently, 90 percent of LocalTalk networks use unshielded or shielded twisted-pair
cable. For Ethernet networks, about 75 percent of installations use thin coaxial cable,
although it's estimated that by 1994, twisted-pair cable will be just as popular as thin
coaxial cable. The majority of Token Ring networks use shielded, twisted-pair cable.

Table 4-1 A comparison of media types

Characteristics	Twisted-pair	Coaxial	Fiber-optic	Infrared light
Distance	Short to moderate	Moderate	Long	Short to moderate
Resistance to interference	Low (shielded slightly better)	Moderate	Very high	Very high
Ease of installation and maintenance	Generally easy to install and maintain	Thick: Requires professional installer or experienced in-house personnel Thin: Generally easy to install	Requires specialized installer	Easy to install and maintain
Associated costs	Low	Low to moderate	High	Moderate
Security: Resistance to illegal monitoring and tapping	Low	Moderate	Very high	Depends on the physical security of the building

5 Topology—The Shape of Your Network

At its most basic, **topology** refers to the physical arrangement of devices and cable in a network. The three most widely used designs for local area networks are bus, star, and ring topologies. But topology is really more than just a matter of geometry—in addition to describing the physical layout of a network, topology is related to the method that devices use to access the network and to send information to each other. On a ring network, for example, each device takes turns transmitting data, whereas on a bus network, devices usually must contend with each other to access the medium.

The network type and media you choose may determine the topology of your network. For example, if you use the Ethernet network type with twisted-pair cable, your network will be laid out in a star. If you select coaxial cable for your Ethernet network instead, your network will be arranged in a bus. Just as you can combine a variety of network types in an internet, so can you combine different network topologies, which means that your internet may consist of several different physical shapes.

This chapter examines each topology and weighs the pros and cons of each.

The bus

A bus topology connects devices in a sequential line, one after the other, as shown in the following figure. A bus always has two distinct ends, each of which must include a **terminating resistor.** Devices are attached along the length of the cable by connectors called **taps** or **drops.** LocalTalk networks using shielded twisted-pair cable and Ethernet networks using coaxial cable are laid out in a bus topology.

Bus topology

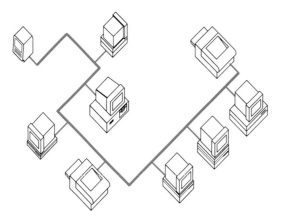

On a bus, there is no central device controlling transmissions on the network. Instead, devices contend with each other to access the medium, a scheme that *distributes* network control. In order to transmit information, devices use a method called **carrier sensing.** Each device "listens" to the medium before transmitting and, if it senses a signal on the medium (which means another device is transmitting), it backs off and tries again later. Transmissions on a bus are broadcast to all devices connected to the medium. To receive a transmission, a device must be able to recognize its own address. (Note that token-passing busses are an exception. Because there are currently no token-passing busses for AppleTalk networks, they are not discussed here.)

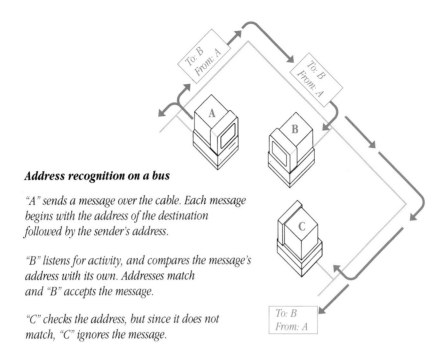

Address recognition on a bus

"A" sends a message over the cable. Each message begins with the address of the destination followed by the sender's address.

"B" listens for activity, and compares the message's address with its own. Addresses match and "B" accepts the message.

"C" checks the address, but since it does not match, "C" ignores the message.

Because devices closest to the sending device receive a stronger signal than devices further away, the transceivers used by the network must tolerate a wide range of signal levels. Signal-strength problems are often handled by limiting the length of the cable segments and the number of devices per segment. On some bus networks, such as coaxial Ethernet networks, amplifying devices (known as *repeaters*—see Chapter 7) are used to connect cable segments.

A distinct advantage of bus networks is that they are easy to configure. The modular design encourages a plug-and-play installation where devices are quickly and easily added to the network. In addition, the distributed nature of a bus provides a certain amount of reliability; the failure of a single device will not affect the rest of the network.

Bus networks do have some disadvantages, however. A break anywhere on the network can disrupt services for all the devices on the network. Problems can be difficult to locate and, depending on the size of the network, the bus may require test equipment to isolate faults. In addition, cable taps may need to be separated by a prescribed distance to avoid signal reflections that can interfere with data transmission.

Carrier sensing: Collision avoidance and detection

Since two devices on a bus could conceivably check the medium at exactly the same time, find no signal, and begin transmitting packets, causing their transmissions to collide, additional precautions are added to carrier sensing. One is called *collision avoidance,* the other is called *collision detection.* In collision avoidance, the protocol attempts to minimize the occurrence of collisions. All nodes wait until the transmission medium has been idle for a specified minimum amount of time plus an additional random period before attempting to transmit. If a collision occurs, the packets are retransmitted. In collision detection, the access protocol specifies a method of detecting collisions and retransmitting the data if a collision has occurred. LocalTalk networks use carrier sensing with collision avoidance. Ethernet networks use carrier sensing with collision detection.

The star

Unshielded, twisted-pair LocalTalk networks (such as Farallon's PhoneNET cable system) and unshielded twisted-pair Ethernet networks allow you to set up your network using a **star** design. A star consists of branches that radiate from a central point, called the *hub.* A branch can contain a single device or several devices arranged in a bus topology. A **passive star** has a fairly low limit on the number of branches allowed and the total length of the cable. An **active star,** which has a controlling device at the hub of the star, allows a greater number of branches and total cable length. The controller in an active star is connected to each device through a dedicated channel, and sends information to the appropriate device rather than broadcasting it to the entire network.

Star networks generally use unshielded twisted-pair cable (telephone wire) as their transmission medium; the center of the star is usually located in a telephone wiring closet. Wires radiate out to users' offices from a wiring distribution block, such as a telephone **punchdown block,** as shown in the following figure.

Active star topology

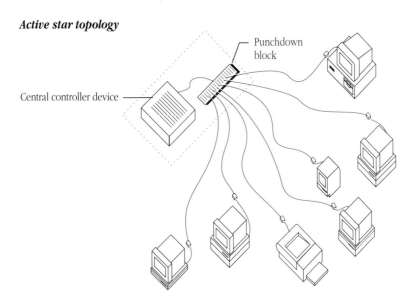

Central controller device

Punchdown block

The greatest strength of star topologies is their ease of maintenance and troubleshooting. Because devices do not share a single cable, it's a relatively straightforward process to isolate faulty cables and devices. If the wiring already exists in offices, it's easy to reconfigure the network by simply reconnecting wires in the telephone wiring closet. Adding or moving devices is not disruptive to the network because each device is isolated from the rest.

If you're planning an active star, you'll need to purchase a central controller device or hub. Probably the biggest weakness of an active star is that if the controller fails, all of the devices connected to it fail as well. Performance in a star is good for moderate amounts of traffic, but the size and capacity of the network varies according to the capability and expandability of the hub. Each controller has a limit to the number of devices that can be connected, so you'll need to add more controllers as your network grows.

The ring

There are several kinds of ring topologies possible on a local area network, including true rings, loops, and star-wired rings. In a **true ring,** devices are connected in a closed circle, with each device wired directly to the next by means of the shortest physical path. Control is distributed, with messages traveling automatically from one device to the next. A **loop** looks the same as a true ring; the difference is that there is a controller directing transmissions on the network. A **star-wired ring,** which is the topology popularized by IBM and used in Token Ring networks, transmits data like a ring, but is shaped like a star.

As shown in the following figure, each device on the star-wired ring is connected to a central wiring concentrator called a **multistation access unit** (MAU). A number of MAUs can be interconnected to form the main ring of a network. All information must travel through the central MAU, but, unlike star networks, this central point does not control network transmissions.

Ring networks usually use **token passing** to control access to the network. A special sequence of data representing the token is passed around the ring from device to device. When a device is holding the token, it has sole access to the cable and can transmit freely without risk of collision. To accept messages, each device must be able to recognize its own address. If the receiving device is the intended destination, it accepts the message; otherwise, it resends the message on to the next device in the ring.

Star-wired ring topology
The token passes from device to device via the central multistation access unit (MAU). The dotted line shows the logical path between stations.

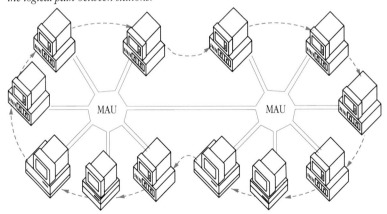

The star-wired ring has several advantages. For one, it is extremely reliable and easy to maintain. The MAU contains automatic bypass relays that enable the ring to continue operating even if a device on the ring fails. The MAU also facilitates maintenance by providing a central location for monitoring and reconfiguration. Another plus is that every device is guaranteed a chance to transmit within a certain period of time—regardless of how busy the network is—so the ring is ideal in situations where network response characteristics must be guaranteed. For example, the ring is useful for real-time applications such as process control and medical monitoring.

On the minus side, star-wired rings can be difficult to install. In addition, the costs for the MAU and for installing the star-wired ring can be quite high and beyond the means of a budget for a small network.

Combining topologies in an internet

In an organization with several connected networks, it's common to encounter a mix of different topologies. For example, one network might be connected to an IBM mainframe through a ring, another network may be set up as a star to take advantage of existing telephone wire, while a third network might be designed as a bus. These different topologies are connected together by using routers, which are discussed in Chapter 7. An example internet combining different topologies is shown in the following figure.

An internet combining different topologies

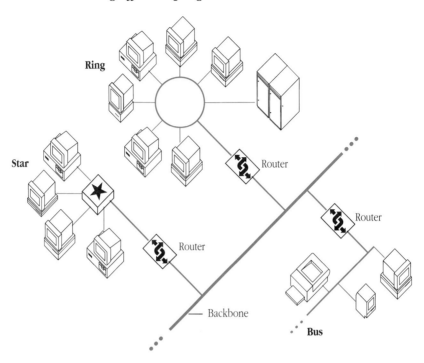

Conclusion

Because the topology of your AppleTalk network will often depend on the network type and media you choose, topology probably won't be the overriding criterion in planning your network. However, by becoming familiar with the characteristics of each topology, you will know what to expect during installation and when you need to reconfigure or troubleshoot the network later on. Each topology has inherent strengths and weaknesses, summarized in Table 5-1.

Table 5-1 A comparison of network topologies

Features	Bus	Star	Star-wired ring
Uses	Ideal for small networks.	Ease of maintenance and troubleshooting.	A good choice for applications that require predictable network response. Part of IBM's Systems Application Architecture (SAA).
Performance	Excellent under light loads; may degrade rapidly if load reaches saturation point.	Good for moderate activity. Performance depends on the capability of the central controller.	Less delay under heavy network load than other topologies. Under light to moderate loads, delays can be longer than other topologies.
Reliability	Failure of one device does not affect the rest of the network. However, a single break can disrupt the network.	Failure of one device does not affect the rest of the network. However, in an active star, if the controller fails, the entire network goes down.	Very reliable. The failure of one device does not affect the rest of the network.
Ease of adding and moving devices	Easy to add or move devices. May cause network disruption.	Easy to reconfigure the network if wire already exists in offices. Adding or removing devices is not disruptive.	Easy to add or move devices without disruption.
Ease of maintenance and troubleshooting	Becomes more difficult as the network grows. Problems can be hard to locate, but are usually easy to repair.	Easy. Because devices do not share a single cable, it is fairly easy to isolate faulty cables and devices.	Generally easy. The MAU provides a central point for monitoring.

6 Network Types

As you learned in Chapter 2, AppleTalk protocols can operate on different network types, including LocalTalk, Ethernet, and Token Ring—each network type supporting a variety of media and topologies. The network type you choose will depend on many factors, such as the amount of activity you expect on your network, the distance that needs to be covered, the number of devices that need to be connected, and budgetary considerations.

This chapter examines each network type and helps you determine which one best fits your organization's requirements.

LocalTalk networks

A LocalTalk network is ideal for small workgroups that generate low to moderate amounts of network activity, generally characterized by shared printing, E-mail, and by file sharing with small numbers of users. (See Chapter 7, "Design Guidelines," for a detailed discussion of network traffic.) LocalTalk provides a transmission speed of 230.4 kilobits per second (Kbps)—about 200 times faster than the data transfer rate between devices using 1200 baud modems.

Because the transceiver for LocalTalk is built into every Macintosh and Apple IIGS computer, most LaserWriter printers, and many peripheral devices, LocalTalk is the most affordable network solution. The software driver for LocalTalk is included as part of the Macintosh and Apple IIGS operating systems.

You can connect Apple IIe computers, MS-DOS computers, and ImageWriter printers to a LocalTalk network by installing the appropriate interface card and software. The Apple II Workstation Card and software is used for the Apple IIe; the PhoneNET Card PC•LocalTalk card (from Farallon Computing) is used for MS-DOS computers; and the LocalTalk Option Card is used for the ImageWriter printer. (Interface cards for some computers are also available from other companies.)

The LocalTalk network type is often used as a starting point for setting up an AppleTalk network. As a LocalTalk network grows, reaching its cable or device limitations, it can be subdivided into two or more LocalTalk networks connected by routers, creating an internet. As the internet grows and has greater performance requirements, LocalTalk networks can be connected to each other through a **backbone network** such as Ethernet (described in the section "AppleTalk Over Ethernet: EtherTalk," later in this chapter).

A LocalTalk network can be used in either bus or star topologies and can use a variety of media, including shielded twisted-pair cable, unshielded twisted-pair cable, and infrared light. The components for these different media are described in the following sections.

Shielded, twisted-pair cable systems

Apple's **LocalTalk cable system** uses inexpensive (typically under $100 per computer), shielded, twisted-pair cable to connect up to 32 devices in a single network. Networks can be connected to support more devices and longer distances. The LocalTalk cable system is always arranged in a bus topology.

LocalTalk cable comes in preassembled kits and in custom wiring kits. A basic kit contains a 2-meter cable (you can also purchase cable in 10-meter or 25-meter lengths), a connector box that connects each device to the cable, and a cable extender (an adapter that joins two cables to form a longer cable and that allows you to reserve a place to add a LocalTalk connector box for another device later on). The custom wiring kit contains a roll of cable and the necessary plugs, cable splicers, and extenders that allow you to create custom-length cables.

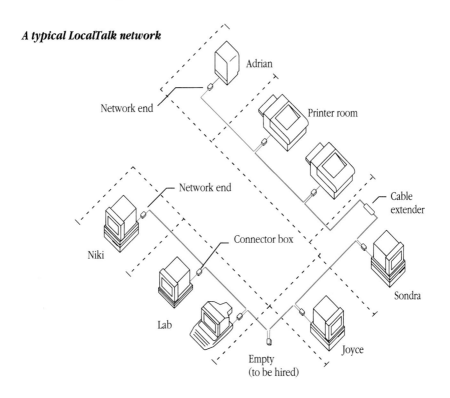

A typical LocalTalk network

Every connector box for the LocalTalk cable system has a built-in resistor that terminates the network. (Note that other types of LocalTalk-compatible networks such as PhoneNet, described in the next section, require you to add terminating resistors to the network.) The connector box at each end of a LocalTalk cable system network must have one empty outlet for proper network termination.

Each device sends information through the LocalTalk connector box, through both cables attached to the box, and out over the bus. It makes no difference where you place devices along the bus; computers, servers, and peripherals such as printers can be located wherever it makes most sense for your network.

Using the LocalTalk cable system, network expansion is quite easy. To add a device to the end of the network, you just plug in a cable and connector box. To add a device between existing network devices, you must temporarily disrupt the network, but the process is the same: add a cable and a connector box. To remove a device, you simply unplug the device from its connector box. The connector box may remain on the network indefinitely without an attached device.

Adding devices...

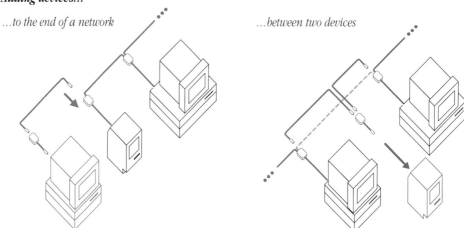

...to the end of a network   ...between two devices

Unshielded twisted-pair cable systems

With the PhoneNET cable system (from Farallon Computing), a LocalTalk network can also use unshielded twisted-pair cable, which makes it possible to use existing telephone wire. Using PhoneNet, a LocalTalk network can extend up to 4000 feet and can be arranged in both bus and star topologies.

The following figure shows a LocalTalk network using unshielded twisted-pair cable in a star topology. The network cables radiate from a hub placed in a central location, usually a telephone wiring closet. The most common configuration uses an active star controller providing a fixed number of ports (usually 12). You should plan to add more controllers as the number of devices on your network grows. In addition to the controller, you need an unshielded twisted-pair connector for each network device.

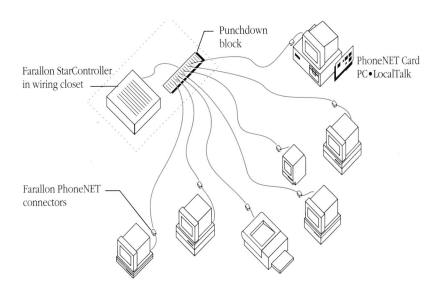

Infrared connections

With infrared technology, such as PhotoLink (from Photonics Corporation), you can set up a LocalTalk network without using cable at all. Infrared installations are suitable for environments that undergo continual rearrangement, such as floors used for a manufacturing process. In an infrared LocalTalk installation, each device is connected to a transceiver that communicates with other devices by bouncing signals off ceilings or walls. Each PhotoLink transceiver has four ports, and each port can connect up to 32 devices.

A disadvantage of infrared networks is that they are not practical in environments where work spaces are closed off by barriers that impede the transmission or reception of the signals.

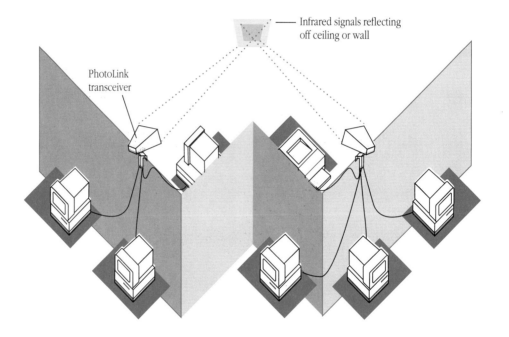

Infrared signals reflecting off ceiling or wall

PhotoLink transceiver

AppleTalk over Ethernet: EtherTalk

AppleTalk protocols can operate on industry-standard **Ethernet** technology, supporting the 802.3 standard defined by the **IEEE (Institute of Electrical and Electronic Engineers).** Ethernet can use a variety of media, transmitting data at 10 megabits per second (Mbps). It is useful for networks that carry heavy traffic; for example, in work environments that have many users or that transfer large files (such as CAD files or other files that include graphics or color), have multi-user database activity, or where applications are typically launched from a file server. Ethernet is also used in environments that require very quick response times.

You can connect most Macintosh computers to an Ethernet network by installing EtherTalk software and an interface card (such as the Apple Ethernet NB Card or Apple Ethernet LC Card) in each computer, or by using an external SCSI box. You can connect LaserWriter printers to an Ethernet network by using a product such as EtherPrint (Dayna Communications).

An Ethernet network can be set up in various ways. Using thin coaxial cable, you can easily connect devices in a bus topology. Ethernet also enables you to connect devices using unshielded, twisted-pair cable (telephone wire), laying out devices in a star-shaped design. In addition, an Ethernet network often functions as a high-speed backbone—using thick coaxial or fiber-optic cable—to connect several LocalTalk networks by means of a router. (See the following figure.) Using Ethernet as a backbone and placing heavily-used devices on the backbone improves access to these devices.

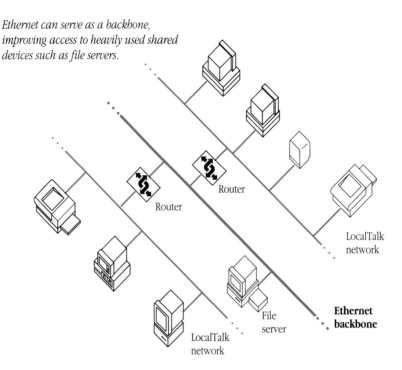

Ethernet can serve as a backbone, improving access to heavily used shared devices such as file servers.

Router

Router

LocalTalk
network

File
server

**Ethernet
backbone**

LocalTalk
network

Devices using EtherTalk software can also communicate over the same Ethernet cable with devices obeying non-AppleTalk protocols, such as TCP/IP and DECnet. This means that, with the appropriate software installed (such as MacTCP®), Ethernet users can communicate with non-AppleTalk devices, such as Sun workstations, and take advantage of non-AppleTalk network services, such as those on a DECnet network, as shown in the following illustration.

Macintosh computers can communicate over
an Ethernet network with non-AppleTalk devices.

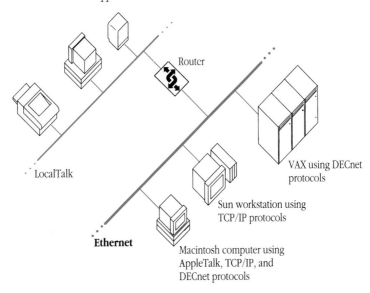

Router

LocalTalk

VAX using DECnet
protocols

Sun workstation using
TCP/IP protocols

Ethernet

Macintosh computer using
AppleTalk, TCP/IP, and
DECnet protocols

The Apple Ethernet Cable System

The **Apple Ethernet Cable System** is a family of products from Apple Computer that
provides connectivity to Ethernet networks. This family of products combines the
modular ease-of-use familiar to LocalTalk users with the high performance and
extensibility of Ethernet networks. All Apple Ethernet products conform to the IEEE
802.3 standard for Ethernet, so they work with Ethernet products from other vendors.

Apple Ethernet media adapters, shown in the following figure, allow you to connect
to any standard Ethernet cable system through the Apple Ethernet port. This port is a
universal connection point provided for your computer through the installation of an
interface card, such as the Apple Ethernet NB Card or Apple Ethernet LC Card. Because
Apple Ethernet separates the transceiver from the interface card, you can use the
appropriate media adapter to switch cable systems without having to replace your
interface card.

Apple Ethernet media adapters

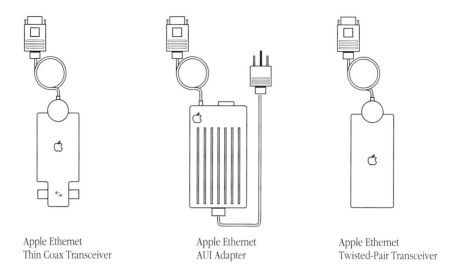

Apple Ethernet
Thin Coax Transceiver

Apple Ethernet
AUI Adapter

Apple Ethernet
Twisted-Pair Transceiver

Thin coax cable systems for Ethernet

The Apple Ethernet Thin Coax Transceiver connects computers and peripheral devices equipped with Apple Ethernet ports to a thin coaxial cable Ethernet network.

The Apple Ethernet Thin Coax Transceiver kit consists of an external transceiver with an Apple Ethernet connector. The kit also includes a 2-meter length of self-terminating cable, which you can use to connect to another transceiver on the network. (You can also purchase cable in 5-meter lengths and 13-meter lengths to connect devices over longer distances.)

The Apple Ethernet Thin Coax Transceiver brings the plug-and-play approach of LocalTalk to thin coax networks. By providing a Thin Coax Transceiver for each device, you can quickly build your own network. You simply connect the network cable to the transceiver and plug the transceiver into a device's Apple Ethernet port. To extend the network, you connect a transceiver to the new device, then use the 2-meter cable to attach to another transceiver already on the network.

Both the Apple Ethernet Thin Coax Transceiver and Apple Ethernet cable are self-terminating, unlike traditional Ethernet hardware. This means that if a cable becomes disconnected for any reason, both halves of the network will remain functional (although the separated networks won't be able to communicate with one another until the cable is reconnected).

In addition to creating a network with all Apple Ethernet components, you can use the Apple Ethernet Thin Coax Transceiver to add devices to existing installations. The transceiver works with any standard thin coax cable system.

Apple Ethernet Thin Coax cable system
A true "plug-and-play" Ethernet network

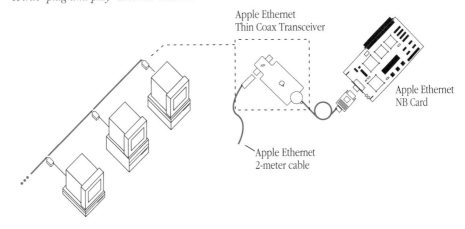

Apple Ethernet
Thin Coax Transceiver

Apple Ethernet
NB Card

Apple Ethernet
2-meter cable

Twisted-pair cable systems for Ethernet

The Apple Ethernet Twisted-Pair Transceiver connects computers and peripheral devices equipped with Apple Ethernet ports to a twisted-pair Ethernet network. The transceiver conforms to the IEEE 802.3 **10BASE-T** standard for implementing Ethernet over unshielded twisted-pair cable.

Ethernet cable systems that use unshielded twisted-pair cable are arranged in a star topology and can take advantage of existing telephone wires that radiate out to work spaces from a central controlling hub. Because the Apple Ethernet Twisted-Pair Transceiver fully supports the 10BASE-T standard, it can be used with any vendor's 10BASE-T hub.

Ethernet twisted-pair cable system

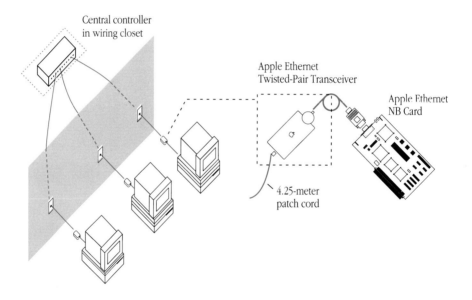

Central controller
in wiring closet

Apple Ethernet
Twisted-Pair Transceiver

Apple Ethernet
NB Card

4.25-meter
patch cord

Thick coax and other cable systems for Ethernet

The Apple Ethernet AUI Adapter enables you to connect a device equipped with an Apple Ethernet port to standard Ethernet transceivers for thick coax, fiber-optic, and other Ethernet media types. The AUI Adapter will work with external transceivers from all companies following the 802.3 AUI (Attachment Unit Interface) specification.

Ethernet cable system for fiber-optic and thick coax

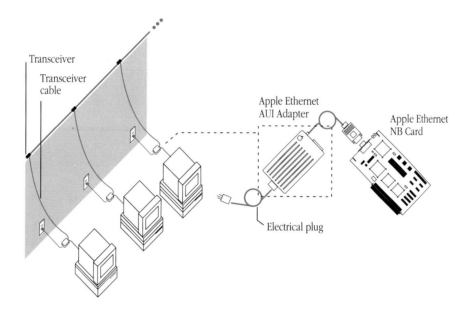

AppleTalk over Token Ring: TokenTalk

A TokenTalk network transmits AppleTalk protocols over industry-standard (IEEE 802.5) **Token Ring** networks. The growing popularity of Token Ring is the result of its compatibility with standard cabling installations and its role in IBM's Systems Application Architecture (SAA), making it ideal for large business installations.

Providing transmission rates of either 4 megabits per second (Mbps) or 16 Mbps, Token Ring can use either shielded twisted-pair cable or unshielded twisted-pair cable. A single network can connect up to 260 devices.

Each device on a Token Ring network is connected to a MAU that is usually located in a wiring closet. A typical MAU provides eight ports for connecting network devices. As your network grows, you can add MAUs to support more devices.

You need TokenTalk software and a Token Ring interface card for each computer that you want to attach to the network. To connect members of the Macintosh II family of computers to Token Ring networks that operate at 4 Mbps, Apple provides the TokenTalk NB Card. This card connects to IBM Type 1 cable (shielded twisted-pair). Other vendors provide media filters for attaching to IBM Type 3 cable (unshielded twisted-pair). You may also purchase interface cards from other companies that allow you to connect a Macintosh SE or SE/30 to a Token Ring network.

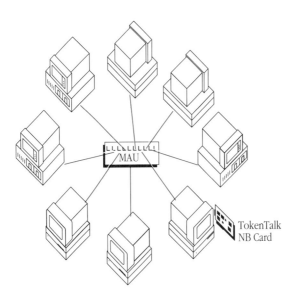

Conclusion

In this chapter, you've learned about the different network types that are supported by the AppleTalk network system—LocalTalk, Ethernet, and Token Ring. These network types target the needs of varying network environments. The following table enables you to compare the features of these network types. Note that AppleTalk protocols can also operate on other types of networks, such as ARCnet, LANSTAR, and IBM baseband networks. For more information on these additional network types, refer to the sources listed in the Appendix.

Table 6-1 A comparison of network types

	Medium	Transmission rate	Topology	Maximum number of devices	Maximum length	Ease of installation
LocalTalk	Shielded twisted-pair	230.4 Kbps	Bus	32	1000 ft.	Easy
	Unshielded twisted-pair (phone wire)	230.4 Kbps	Bus Passive star	20–40 Varies	2000 ft. 4000 ft. (sum of branches)	Easy Requires installer
			Active star	254	3000 ft./branch	Requires installer
	Infrared light	230.4 Kbps	NA	128 per transceiver	Transceivers must be within 70-ft. diameter	Easy
Ethernet	Thick coaxial	10 Mbps	Bus	100/segment 1024/network	8250 ft.	Requires installer
	Thin coaxial	10 Mbps	Bus	40/segment 1024/network	3300 ft.	Easy with Apple Ethernet product
	Twisted-pair	10 Mbps	Star	1024	330 ft. from hub to device	Requires installer
	Fiber optic	10 Mbps	Bus	1024	14,256 ft.	Requires installer
Token Ring	Shielded twisted-pair	4 /16 Mbps	Star-wired ring	260/ring	990 ft. from MAU to device	Usually requires installer
	Unshielded twisted-pair	4 /16 Mbps	Star-wired ring	72/ring	330 ft. from MAU to device	Usually requires installer

7 Design Guidelines

When you begin planning your network design, a number of questions may spring to mind immediately. Where should shared resources, such as printers and servers, be placed? Can users be set up into a single network or is it necessary to create several connected networks? What kind of computer should be used as a file server? This chapter provides guidelines for questions such as these and includes the following design topics:

- how to plan for network activity
- how to determine shared resource needs
- how to expand a single network
- when it makes sense to create two or more connected networks
- how to determine which device to use to connect networks together
- dividing your internet into zones
- when to use a backbone network
- where to locate shared resources
- creating a network map

Planning for network traffic

One of the main factors to consider when designing your network is the kind and amount of network activity or **traffic** that your network will carry. Network traffic is generated any time two devices communicate. This means that whenever one device attempts to access another device, such as a computer accessing a printer, file server, or another computer, traffic is created on the network. Packet volume is an indication of the total traffic on the network at any given time. The more frequently devices communicate over the network, the greater the number of packets sent, and the greater the volume of network traffic.

When a network is designed and maintained properly, it is generally **transparent** to users. This means that users are unaware of the communication taking place between devices that enable the network to function efficiently. With a well-designed network, for example, users can quickly download information from the file server and print without delay. However, if a network is not properly designed, **network performance** may decline, causing delays in network services—and users will come running to you to fix their problems!

There are two types of traffic generated on a network: **overhead traffic** and **user-generated traffic.** Overhead traffic is generated by network devices and comes from such sources as

- routers updating routing tables throughout the internet
- E-mail message alerts
- file server volumes mounted on user desktops

User-generated traffic is created by user requests and constitutes the bulk of network traffic. It results from such activities as

- computer startup
- using the Chooser
- printing documents
- accessing the file server

- sending and receiving E-mail
- using remote access devices such as shared network modems

After your network is up and running, there are some steps you can take to minimize the amount of overhead traffic. For example, if many users mount server volumes on their computers automatically when they start up (whether they use the server or not), you may have a great deal of unnecessary overhead traffic. To alleviate this problem, you can ask users to log on to servers only when they plan on using them. During the design phase, however, you'll focus on anticipating user-generated traffic, discussed in the next section.

Creating a balanced network

In many ways, network traffic is analogous to the traffic on streets and freeways. Like a freeway, the efficiency of a network depends on free-flowing traffic. If the network becomes congested, bottlenecks can occur, often resulting in performance degradation.

Your primary goal in network design is to ensure a balance of network traffic so that bottlenecks don't occur. One of the main considerations will be the *kinds* of network functions each user will be performing. The network usage level of any user can be generally classed as low, medium, or high. While there are no actual rules that specify the number of devices per type of usage, analyzing usage levels will give you a good idea of what kind of traffic to expect, helping you to plan a balanced network.

The following chart provides some guidelines on network usage levels and helps you evaluate the kind of activity users will generate. As you can see from this chart, printing generally creates low levels of network traffic. A computer sends a print job to the printer or server, and the communication ends. Launching an application from the file server, on the other hand, generates high levels of traffic because information is continuously sent back and forth over the network between the file server and the user's computer.

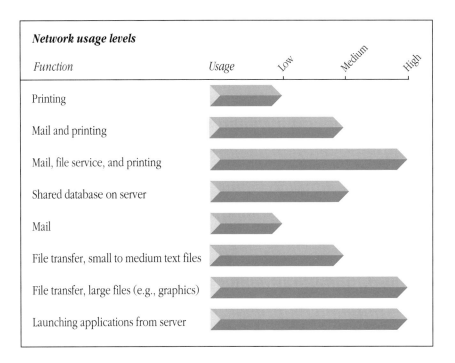

Note that the number of users taking part in network activity at a given time will also affect the overall level of network traffic. For example, the greater the number of people accessing a shared database on the server simultaneously, the greater your traffic will be.

Once you've analyzed the usage levels of network users and the total number of users likely to engage in specific network activities, compare network groupings (such as departments) with this list to see which groups are likely to generate high traffic. You can use these results to design a balanced network layout and to assign network resources to users.

For example, if you have 30 users who will be printing short documents and exchanging E-mail, you can readily group those users into a single LocalTalk network. It would be unwise, however, to group 30 high-usage individuals into one LocalTalk network, since each LocalTalk network has a limit of about 32 devices. Instead, you may opt to balance network activity by dividing this group into two LocalTalk networks, connected by a router, or to use Ethernet instead. (See the section "Extending and Connecting Networks" later in this chapter for a discussion of when and how to connect networks.)

If you're using LocalTalk, a safe guideline is to consider 16–20 medium-usage devices as a full network. It's good policy to underload LocalTalk networks in an initial internet design; this will accommodate growth by making it possible to add to each network rather than creating additional networks.

In Chapter 10, you'll learn how to monitor your network traffic and optimize performance as your network changes and grows.

Determining shared resource needs

Once you know which services and applications will be used on your network, you can determine your shared resource requirements. For example, if you've decided to use centralized AppleShare file service, what kind of computer will you need as a server: will a Macintosh Classic® be adequate to meet your needs or will you need to use one of the higher-performance Macintosh II family of computers? Should you run more than one network service on the same server? How much shared disk space will each user require on each server? How many servers or printers will you need?

Many factors affect the shared resource requirements for your network, including the type of services and applications being used, the number of users, the anticipated amount of use (moderate? heavy?), and the amount of general network activity you have on your network. Some of the basic decisions you need to make about shared resources include:

- which network type to use (LocalTalk, Ethernet, or Token Ring)
- the number of shared devices you need (such as file servers and printers)
- the type of computer to use as a server
- the type of disk drive to use
- whether to run multiple services on the same server
- the amount of shared disk space you need (number and size of volumes)
- the amount of server memory you need

Your main goal in assessing shared resource needs is to deliver a sufficient level of service and performance to network users. When shared resources adequately meet the needs of your users, they will receive network services without any noticeable delays. However, inadequate resources will become apparent when users begin experiencing slowdowns in network services.

The following sections provide some rules of thumb to help guide you through some of these shared resource decisions. Bear in mind that these are not hard and fast rules. As you can imagine, there are many variables involved in determining shared resource needs. The best approach is to make an educated guess and then make any necessary adjustments as the need arises. As you gain experience as a network administrator and become familiar with the ins and outs of your own network's operation, you'll become more adept at estimating your requirements.

The Macintosh computer is used here as the basis for discussing server performance, but the concepts discussed apply to other server platforms as well.

The network type

The network type determines how fast information moves from one device to another (such as between a computer and a server) and has the most significant impact on network performance. If your network and server activity will be moderate, LocalTalk may deliver ample performance. However, Ethernet and Token Ring deliver significantly higher network performance levels and may be appropriate for your network environment. Accessing a file server on a Token Ring network can provide about four times the performance of accessing the same file server over a LocalTalk network, while an Ethernet network can typically provide six to eight times the performance of a LocalTalk network.

Shared devices—how many?

The number of shared devices you need is determined, in part, by usage levels. A large accounting group doing heavy database work may need its own file server. A publications department that does constant printing of long documents probably needs several printers. When estimating the number of shared printers you need, consider such factors as printer speed and output and the number and size of printing jobs. When determining how many servers you need, consider that a network service may have limits to the number of users that can simultaneously access the service. For instance, the AppleShare File Server allows up to 50 users to log on to the file server at the same time.

Note that some network services can run simultaneously on the same server computer, reducing the number of servers you may need. See the section "Running Multiple Services on One Server" later in this chapter for more information.

The type of computer to use as a server

If you're using an Ethernet network, the type of computer you use as a file server can affect the server's performance. This has not been found to be true on LocalTalk and Token Ring networks. For these networks, performance is limited by the network itself, not by the choice of computer used as the server.

In general, the more powerful the server on an Ethernet network, the better the server performance will be. Consider how your file server will be used when deciding which computer you need. If your file server will be used by 15 people for activities that generate low to moderate amounts of traffic—such as file transfer with small text files or infrequent launching of applications—a lower-cost Macintosh computer will probably deliver adequate server performance. However, if your server will be used by the same number of people for large file transfers or heavy multi-user database access, you'll probably want to use a higher-performance Macintosh computer. (See Table 7-1 for some general guidelines on AppleShare File Server configurations.)

The type of disk drive to use

The type of hard drive you use can make a difference in server performance, especially under a heavy load or when transferring large files. For faster disk access speeds and improved server performance, use a high-performance disk drive.

Running multiple services on one server

Running multiple services on the same server is a highly cost-effective use of server hardware. However, if your network demands the least possible risk from degradation in server performance, it may not be appropriate.

A very common configuration is to run print service and file service on the same Macintosh server. An AppleShare print server generates relatively low levels of input/output traffic, so server performance is less likely to be degraded by its concurrent use with other network services. However, if you run routing software (such as the AppleTalk Internet Router) concurrently with file service, users may notice a slowdown in server performance, particularly if the router is sending large amounts of traffic to another network.

If you run multiple services, you may need additional memory on the server to deliver adequate performance to network users (see the section "The Amount of Server Memory"). You may want to experiment with multiple services to determine whether the resulting server performance is appropriate for your needs.

Shared disk space

Another factor to consider is the amount of hard disk storage required for each server. For file service, you can get a general idea of how much storage space you'll need by learning what kinds of applications and files will be stored on the server. Some applications, such as graphics programs, spreadsheet programs, and high-end word-processing software, can be very large. In addition, the files created from these applications may also use up a lot of disk space. Short text files or smaller applications will naturally use less storage space on the server.

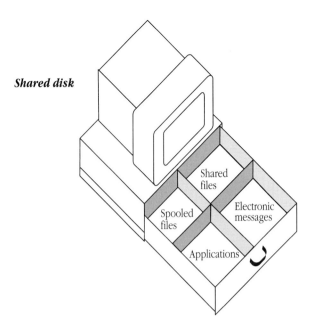

Shared disk

Shared files

Electronic messages

Spooled files

Applications

One other point to keep in mind when determining how much shared disk space you need is whether you need any separate volumes for security reasons. For instance, you may want to set up a separate volume for high-security financial data to make the information inaccessible to others using the server.

If you're running spooler software on the server, you'll need to allocate adequate disk space for spooled files. Consider such factors as the number of users and the average size of documents to be spooled. Spooling typically requires a minimum of ten megabytes of disk space. However, this number can vary considerably depending upon the size of the spooled files.

If you're running an electronic mail application, allocate space for storing messages and for overhead message processing. For messaging, disk space depends on the E-mail application being used, the number of people using the system, their method of access, and how long you store messages on the server (30 days is common). E-mail typically requires a large amount of disk space. In addition, many mail programs require that the space be available on one single disk rather than on multiple disks. Consult the manual that came with your mail application for specific disk space requirements.

The amount of server memory

Adding memory to a server can improve its performance and functionality. Additional memory can support a greater number of simultaneous users and helps to support other services on a file server such as print spooling, electronic mail, and router services. Added memory not only allows more services to run simultaneously, but also allows these services to run more efficiently.

Table 7-1 AppleShare File Server configuration guidelines *(for file service only)*

Usage level	Number of concurrent users	Recommended server configuration
Light to moderate use*	Up to 10	Macintosh Classic or Macintosh SE/30 with 2 MB RAM and 40 MB hard disk storage
	Up to 30	Macintosh SE/30 with 4 MB RAM and 80 MB hard disk storage
	Up to 50	Macintosh II† with 4 MB RAM and 100+ MB hard disk storage
	Over 50	Configure 2 servers
Heavy use‡	Up to 20	Macintosh II with 4 MB RAM and 80 MB hard disk storage
	Up to 35	Macintosh II with 4 MB RAM and 100+ MB hard disk storage
	Over 35	Macintosh II with 4 MB RAM and 160+ MB disk storage or configure 2 servers

* Assumes that the server will be used mainly for storing small applications (or few large applications) and text files.

† Refers to one of the Macintosh II family of computers.

‡ Assumes that the server will be used to store many space-intensive applications and files, such as large spreadsheets, graphics, and multi-user databases.

Extending and connecting networks

When designing your network, you may find that you need to extend a single network or divide the network into two or more connected *subnetworks.* Connection devices such as repeaters, bridges, routers, and gateways (discussed fully in the next section) extend networks or provide the link between individual networks, enabling many users to communicate and share resources with one another.

The following situations commonly call for extending or connecting networks:

- *Enlarging a network that has reached its maximum length or number of devices.* If you've reached the specified device or cable length limits of a network, you may need to extend the network. For example, if you're using LocalTalk cable and need to extend the cable beyond the specified 1000-foot limit, you would need to use a connection device.

- *Linking two or more existing networks in your organization.* It's not unusual for networks to be installed in an organization for different reasons and at different times. The result? Separate networks that don't communicate. Connection devices can link these networks together, allowing users on each network to access network services on the entire internet.

- *Connecting different network types or networks using different protocols.* A common reason for connecting networks is to link different network types, such as LocalTalk and Ethernet, each using different connection methods and transmission media. Or you may need to link your AppleTalk network to a network running an entirely different set of protocols, such as DECnet or TCP/IP.

- *Maintaining a satisfactory level of network performance.* In a high-traffic network, performance can be increased significantly by dividing the network into subnetworks, each with a low demand for the resources of another subnetwork. A logical way to divide an existing network is along natural divisions within the organization. For example, networks are commonly divided by department or by groups that have shared requirements. By partitioning the network into largely self-contained subnetworks, you can minimize the amount of traffic flowing between them and maintain higher levels of performance on each subnetwork.

- *Isolating a single group generating high traffic.* When one group of users generates a large amount of network traffic, performance may decline on the entire network. For example, several users performing frequent, high-volume printing and file sharing can cause network congestion for all other users on the same network.

  When designing your network layout, you can plan for such high-traffic groups ahead of time by isolating these users in a network of their own. If your network is already in place, you can use the same traffic-isolation technique, dividing one large network into two smaller networks.

- *Accommodating different user requirements.* If users' needs for network resources vary greatly, you may want to consider creating two networks linked by a connection device. In this way, the special interests of each group may be better satisfied.

- *Restricting access to sensitive information.* You may decide that sensitive or important information—such as product development plans or personnel files—can be better safeguarded and supervised by placing the information in a separate network. Even though users in other networks can access devices on the "secure" network, you can set up certain servers that have restricted access.

- *Creating zones for efficient network organization.* **Zones** are logical divisions within an internet that enable an administrator to balance the number of network services presented to users. See "Dividing Your Internet Into Zones" later in this chapter for a discussion of zones.

Which connection device do you need?

Four kinds of devices are used to extend or connect networks:

- repeaters
- bridges
- routers
- gateways

The device you choose depends on what kind of connection services you need, as described in the following sections.

Repeaters

A **repeater** is a piece of hardware about the size of a modem. It is commonly used to add another length of cable to a network, extending the cable beyond its recommended maximum length. As a transmission signal travels through the network cable, the signal becomes weakened. The repeater amplifies and retransmits this signal, effectively enabling it to travel beyond the normal limitations of the cable.

A repeater can be very helpful if, for example, you have a few users on a LocalTalk network whose offices are isolated from the rest of their group, requiring a total cable length greater than the 1000 feet allowed by LocalTalk. The repeater enables you to connect those users to the network rather than creating another, separate, network.

You can also use a repeater to add devices to a network cable; however, there are two important points to keep in mind. One, repeaters *do not isolate traffic.* When you add a repeater to your network, the result is one larger network. The traffic that results from adding more devices can quickly degrade performance on the entire network. Two, be aware of the recommended device limitations of each network type. It would be unwise, for example, to use a repeater to go well beyond the 32-device limitation of LocalTalk (using the LocalTalk cable system), since performance would rapidly suffer. However, if you're using Ethernet, which can accommodate a large number of devices, a repeater may be a good choice for adding more devices.

Repeaters *enable a cable to be extended beyond its recommended length.*

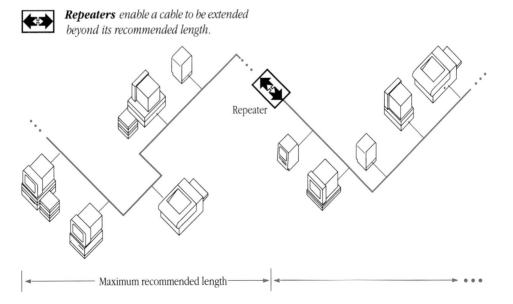

Repeater

Maximum recommended length

Bridges

A **bridge** can be used to join two networks of the same network type (such as two Ethernet networks or two Token Ring networks). The networks can use different types of media, such as fiber-optic or coaxial cable. Note that there are currently no bridges available to connect LocalTalk networks; routers are used instead (see the next section for a discussion of routers).

Unlike a repeater, which simply retransmits all data onto the connected cable segment, bridges can interpret data addresses. This means that bridges can *isolate* traffic on each network, sending only those packets across the bridge specifically destined for the other network. (Note that bridges do not typically isolate **broadcast traffic,** which results from such activities as using the Chooser.)

Bridges can be dedicated, self-contained devices or computers running appropriate bridging software. Because the networks connected by a bridge are not identified by network numbers or zone names (unlike routers), installing and administering a bridge is usually quite easy. Bridges provide administrators with information about network activity levels and error statistics, which are helpful in monitoring the network.

 Bridges *are used to connect networks together. Devices see the previously separate networks as one single, larger network.*

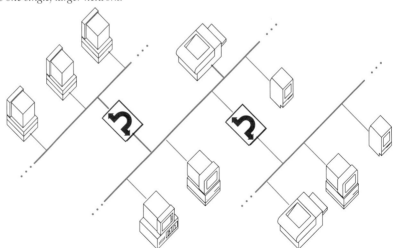

Connection devices and the OSI model

Connection devices perform network functions that involve different layers in the hierarchical OSI model. In this hierarchy, as you may recall from Chapter 2, each layer represents a separate level of network function. Network connection devices perform functions that may involve one or more of these layers. For example, repeaters—very simple hardware devices—make use of the protocols in just the physical layer, whereas gateways—sophisticated translators between different protocol architectures—use the greatest range of networking protocols.

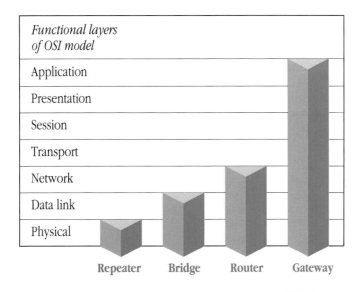

Functional layers
of OSI model

Application	
Presentation	
Session	
Transport	
Network	
Data link	
Physical	

Repeater   Bridge   Router   Gateway

Routers

Routers can connect networks of the same network type (such as two LocalTalk networks) or of different network types (such as an Ethernet network and a Token Ring network). Routers enable the connected networks to retain separate identities with their own unique network numbers, and they can selectively route data along the most efficient path possible. This ensures faster traffic flow and can automatically provide for detours if a connection is broken along the path.

Routers are often used to isolate areas of high traffic from lower-traffic areas for optimum network performance. They also enable you to partition an internet into zones, which make it easier for users to locate and access network services. In addition, routers (like bridges) provide administrators with information about network activity levels and error statistics, which are helpful in monitoring the network.

Routers can be hardware- or software-based. A hardware-based router is a dedicated box whose only function is routing. It is generally a self-contained device, without a monitor or keyboard, designed to be used only as a router. A software-based router operates on a general-purpose computer such as a Macintosh. It can be used as either a dedicated or nondedicated router, depending on the level of performance your network requires. A dedicated router is a computer which, when running routing software, is used for no other purpose. A nondedicated router operates on a computer that can be used concurrently for other network services as well. If your router is sending large amounts of traffic to other networks or if you need the highest possible performance from your router, a dedicated router is the better choice.

Each router on an internet maintains a **routing table** (shown in the following figure) that lists all networks and routers in the internet. The routing table enables routers to determine the most efficient route for each packet of data.

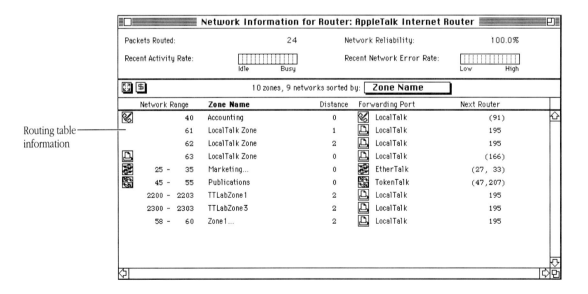

Routing table information

The routing table serves as a logical map of the internet. It lists the network number (or network range) for each network, associated zone names, the address of the next router in the path to a given destination network, and the distance to other networks, measured in **hops.** A hop is a unit count between networks on an internet, and means "one router away." Each router uses this routing table to determine where (and whether) to forward a data packet.

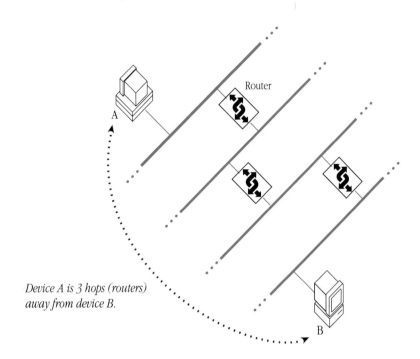

Device A is 3 hops (routers) away from device B.

Routers can be used in the following ways.

- *To connect local networks:* A **local router** is used to connect two or more networks in close proximity.

- *To connect remote networks:* A **half-router** (or *remote router*) is used to connect two or more remote networks over a long-distance telecommunications link. Each network is connected to a router, which in turn is connected to a modem.

- *To connect networks to a backbone:* A **backbone router** can be either a local router or a half-router. The router is used to connect networks through a backbone network, allowing you to link networks in a nonserial manner. This configuration minimizes the number of hops between networks (a network is no more than two hops from another network) and thereby improves performance. (See "When to Use a Backbone" later in this chapter for more information on backbone networks.)

A **router** maintains a logical map of networks in an internet and can route data along the most efficient path.

Local networks

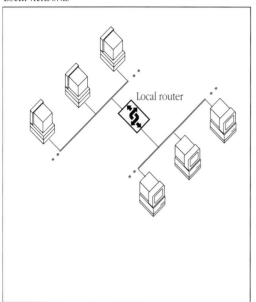

Local router

Remote networks

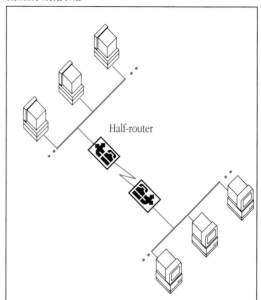

Half-router

Networks connected to a backbone

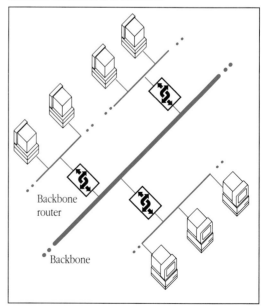

Backbone router

Backbone

Because routers are inherently more intelligent than bridges, they do require more administration time. When you set up a router, you must identify each connected network with a *network number* or *network range* (see "Assigning Network Numbers and Ranges" later in this chapter), and you also need to specify zone names. Routers generate more overhead traffic than bridges since they are continually updating the routing tables of all routers in the internet.

Where to place a router

Each internet is, in some ways, unique. The connected networks can differ in size, layout, and type. As long as a router is properly connected, there are no absolute rules that govern its placement in the internet. You can place a router at any point along the length of a network. It isn't necessary to connect networks end-to-end with a router between each network. The figure below shows examples of possible router locations.

You can place a router at any point along the length of a network.

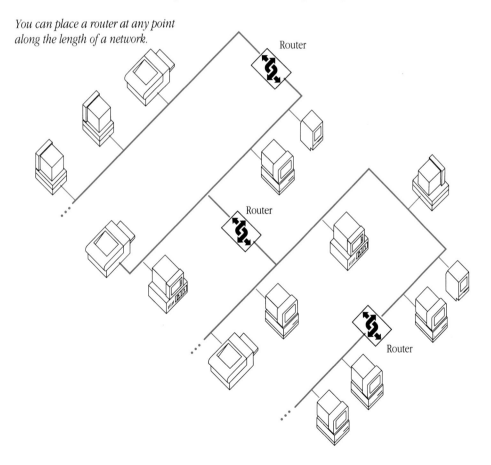

Creating redundant routes

Where possible, try to create duplicate routes to each individual network in an internet. Using this technique, called **redundant routing,** you can prevent networks from getting cut off from the rest of the internet if a break occurs on one of their access routes.

In the figure below, a router has been added to the internet, resulting in redundant connections between networks. The additional router provides an alternate access route between any two networks, thereby improving network reliability; it also reduces the number of hops between some of the networks.

Be aware that if you create redundant routes with the same number of hops, troubleshooting can be more difficult, because it may be hard to figure out which path the packets are following.

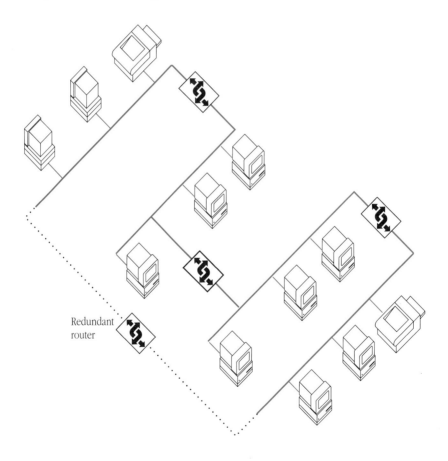

Redundant router

Dividing your internet into zones

During router setup, you can arrange devices into logical groupings called **zones** that *conceptually* partition the internet. There are two main reasons to create zones: to make it easier for users to locate devices, and to facilitate the creation of departmental workgroups that may reside on different physical networks.

Internets can contain many hundreds of shared resources, such as printers and file servers. If users had to sort through a list of all these devices, the process would be overwhelmingly long and cumbersome. Dividing the internet into zones is a much preferred alternative, enabling users to view the devices within a single zone rather than those on the entire internet.

Zones also enable administrators to group users into a single zone regardless of where they are physically located. A group of users assigned to the same zone can efficiently locate the network resources in that zone. This is convenient in situations where members of a department or workgroup reside in different physical areas. This also lets administrators change zone groupings without having to change any physical connections.

If you do set up users so that they are in the same zone, but reside on different networks, be aware that this may cause areas of high traffic on the internet. For example, in the following diagram, if a user in Zone B on the Token Ring network needs to access the file server in Zone B on the LocalTalk network, this will cause traffic on both the intervening Ethernet network and the LocalTalk network. Especially in large internets, you should consider grouping all the users on one network into a single zone to isolate traffic within that network.

Zones have no physical boundaries or size limits. A zone can include one device, several devices, or all of the devices on the entire internet.

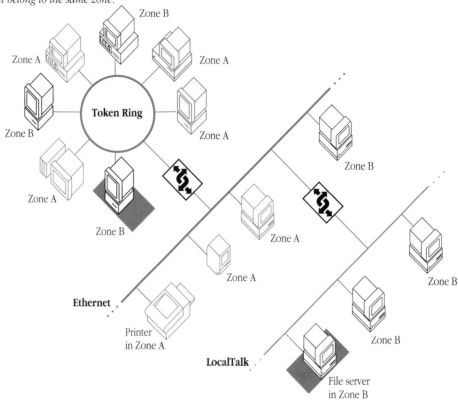

Users connected to different physical networks can belong to the same zone.

Zone B

Zone A

Zone A

Token Ring

Zone B

Zone A

Zone B

Zone A

Zone B

Zone A

Zone A

Zone B

Ethernet

Printer
in Zone A

Zone B

LocalTalk

File server
in Zone B

Zone names and zone lists

When you set up a router, you can associate one or more **zone names** with each network connected to the router. The name identifies the zone to users through the Chooser and is used in various router displays. It's a good idea to keep zone names short and simple and to make them meaningful to users. A common method is to use departmental names or locations, such as Personnel, Engineering, or Finance East and Finance West.

A single LocalTalk network can be associated with only *one* zone name; all of the devices on that network belong to this one zone. A single Ethernet or Token Ring network can have *multiple* zone names, which means that the devices on the network can belong to different zones. These multiple zone names are referred to as a **network zone list,** which contains one or more zone names available to nodes on that network. During router setup, you specify the default zone for each device. You (or any other user) can change the zone to which a device belongs through the Network control panel (or the Control Panel if you're using Macintosh system software earlier than version 7.0).

If only one zone is defined for the entire internet (or if no zones are defined), *all* network services in the internet are presented in each Macintosh user's Chooser window, and *no* zone name is displayed.

Assigning network numbers and ranges

When you use a router to connect networks, you need to identify each network by assigning it a unique number or range of numbers. (As with zone name assignments, this is done during router setup.) LocalTalk networks are always identified by a single network number. Ethernet and Token Ring networks are identified by a **network range.** The network number or range must be unique in the internet. No two networks can have the same number and no two network ranges can overlap or have any network numbers in common.

The network range is a series of contiguous network numbers, such as 1–10. Each number in a network range is a network identifier that can be associated with up to 254 devices. The size of the network range determines the maximum number of AppleTalk devices on the physical network. For example, a network having the range 1–10 could contain up to 10 x 254 devices, or 2,540 devices. If an Ethernet or Token Ring network is never expected to require more than 254 devices, you can assign a range that contains a single number, such as 100–100.

When assigning a network range, be sure the size of the range allows for ample network growth. For example, in a network containing 500 devices, the range 1–2 would accommodate current needs (2 x 254 devices = 508), but would only allow 8 additional node addresses for future growth. Exceeding this level of growth would require you to shut down the router and assign a new, larger network range, disrupting network services to users.

The recommended guideline in choosing a network range is to allow capacity for at least twice the current number of nodes (more, if rapid growth is anticipated). Since an AppleTalk internet supports up to 65,279 network addresses, or over 16 million possible node addresses (65,279 x 254 nodes), it's possible to assign oversized network ranges and still have sufficient addresses for a *very* large internet. For further flexibility in your internet setup, when assigning network ranges, allow wide margins between the ranges you select. For example, if you assign a range of 100–110 to a network, you may want to start the next range with network number 120 rather than network number 111. If your internet has relatively few networks, margins between network ranges can be very large.

◆ **Note** Network ranges are part of the extended addressing capabilities of **AppleTalk Phase 2.** To learn more about the capabilities of AppleTalk Phase 2, refer to *Inside AppleTalk* (second edition), the *AppleTalk Phase 2 Introduction and Upgrade Guide,* and *The Advantages of AppleTalk Phase 2.* See the Appendix for information on how to obtain these publications. ◆

Although there are no rules for numbering networks, it's useful to observe a consistent network numbering scheme—especially in large and fast-growing internets. One such scheme involves assigning a location code or department code to the digits in a network number. The following figure illustrates how a network numbering system can help to identify networks in an orderly way.

Sample network range: 12345–12399

| 1 | 2 | 3 | 45–99 |

Site location (headquarters, field office, etc.) ──────
Building ──────
Floor ──────
Network range ──────

A network numbering system serves several purposes:

- It facilitates the assignment of network numbers when new networks are created.
- It identifies each network in a way that is meaningful to you. For instance, you can look at a routing table and immediately associate the network numbers with their physical locations (such as "building 2, third floor").
- It avoids potential network numbering conflicts that can arise with duplicate numbers.

Keep track of your network numbers and ranges by recording them in a logbook, in an electronic spreadsheet, or on your network map.

Gateways

The fourth kind of connection device—a **gateway**—is a combination of hardware and software that connects an AppleTalk network with a network using non-AppleTalk protocols, such as TCP/IP or DECnet. Gateways serve as translators between these otherwise incompatible network protocols. A gateway is not necessarily used to make a network larger; its primary purpose is to overcome differences between connected networks. The gateway interprets network-related information in a data transmission, such as addressing and routing instructions, then translates this information into the format of the protocols running on the connected network.

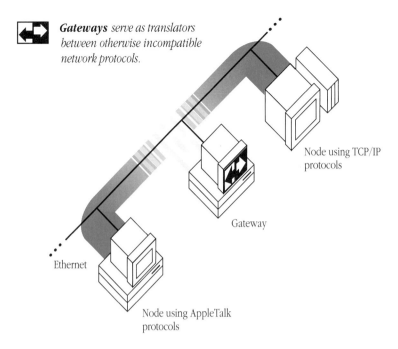

Gateways *serve as translators between otherwise incompatible network protocols.*

Node using TCP/IP protocols

Gateway

Ethernet

Node using AppleTalk protocols

When to use a backbone

If you are planning an internet, you'll find that a **backbone network** is a very useful part of an efficient network layout. The primary function of a backbone is to transport information between other (often slower-speed) networks. A backbone is like a superhighway. It alleviates cross-network traffic congestion, providing each connected network with a more direct route to every other network in the internet. With a well-planned backbone network, data can be sent through a minimal number of routers to reach the destination network.

It's especially useful to create a backbone network to connect many separate networks or to connect networks that aren't physically contiguous. A backbone is often used to connect networks on different floors of a building or in different buildings. In addition, you can connect network devices directly to a backbone, permitting faster access to heavily used devices such as file servers.

Example A: *without a backbone*

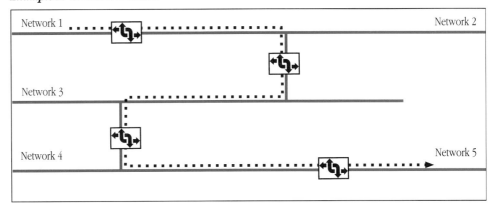

Example B: *with a backbone*

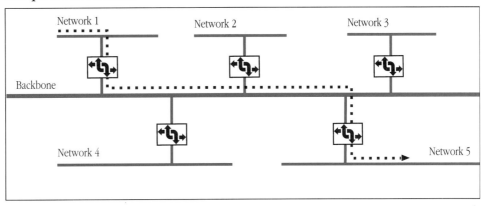

In the preceding figure, Example A shows five networks connected serially by routers, with no backbone. To get from Network 1 to Network 5, a packet would need to travel four hops and would have to contend with network traffic on three intervening networks—which may themselves be slower networks. In contrast, in Example B, the same transmission would need to travel only two hops, with the backbone network in between. (Network performance can be further enhanced if the backbone is a high-speed network such as Ethernet, as discussed in the next section.)

Selecting the backbone network type

Any network type that can be connected to a router can be set up as a backbone. However, since the object of a backbone is to enhance performance—and since the backbone may be used as a thoroughfare for many connected networks—it's desirable for the backbone network to transmit data at a fast rate.

For example, any type of network can provide the efficiency of fewer hops between networks, but an Ethernet or Token Ring backbone also provides a high transmission speed. The backbone network type you select should take into account the usage level and performance needs of your own internet.

Connecting networks of different speeds

Since you can combine different network types in an internet, you need to consider *where* it would be most advantageous to place higher-speed networks in the layout of your internet. When possible, use faster networks in a busy route between other networks, as illustrated in the following figure.

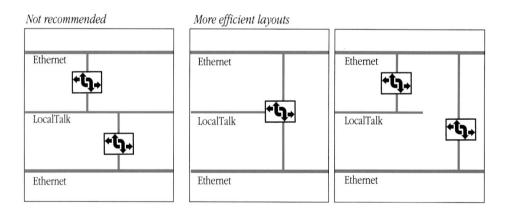

When connecting networks of different speeds, consider that most lower-cost routers (including the AppleTalk Internet Router) do not distinguish the *speed* of a network when selecting the most direct route to a destination. Instead, these routers select the route with the least number of *hops*. If you have a lower-cost router, wherever redundant routes exist, try to place fewer hops in the faster network so that this is the path selected. You may want to consider eliminating redundant routes in which the number of hop counts will cause the router to select the slower-speed route.

Where to place shared resources

How do you determine where it would be most efficient to place shared resources? If you have a single network, it doesn't matter where you place printers and servers from a *network performance* standpoint. However, you *will* want to consider factors such as convenience and security. Shared printers should be easily accessible by network users. You may want to place servers close to you for administrative purposes or in an isolated area for security reasons (see Chapter 9 for a discussion of security).

If you have two or more connected networks, there is one basic, common-sense rule about where to place shared resources: always try to place them on the same network as the people most frequently using them. Avoid placing routers or bridges between users and the devices they share. This will cause unnecessary traffic over networks that do not use the devices or that use them infrequently. If your internet includes a backbone network, consider locating devices shared equally by many networks on that backbone. (See the following examples.)

Poor network design

If many users on Network B need to use the modem server on Network A, unnecessary traffic will be generated on Network A.

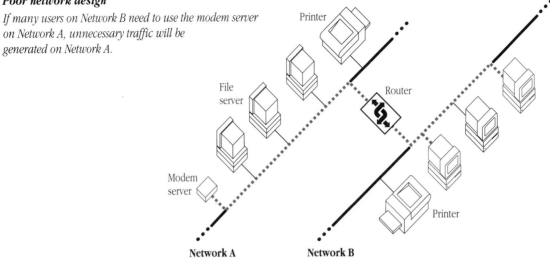

Recommended network design

To isolate traffic on each network, Network B has been given its own modem server.

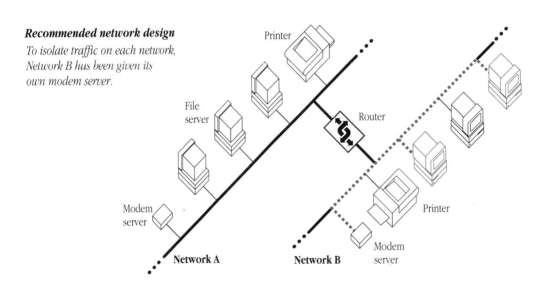

Placing shared devices on a backbone

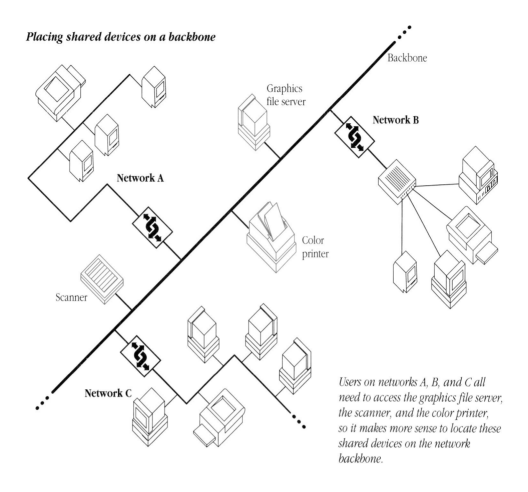

Backbone

Graphics
file server

Network B

Network A

Color
printer

Scanner

Network C

Users on networks A, B, and C all
need to access the graphics file server,
the scanner, and the color printer,
so it makes more sense to locate these
shared devices on the network
backbone.

Creating a network map

When you're ready to detail the physical layout of your network, you'll start by drawing a **network map.** The map is a graphic representation of your network and is an essential planning tool. It will assist you in designing the initial network layout, helping you to figure out where it's best to place printers and file servers, how a network should be partitioned into zones, where a router would be most optimal, and where cable needs to be installed.

The network map is also an important management tool, helping you keep track of changes to your network in an organized way and making it easier to troubleshoot problems that arise (as you'll see in Chapter 11). For example, if several users tell you that they can no longer use a shared printer, the network map can reveal the point where their computers are cut off from the rest of the network. The importance of network maps becomes more obvious as networks grow into internets and are complicated by routers, gateways, backbone networks, and multiple floors or buildings.

There are many kinds of network maps. The most commonly used ones are *schematic maps, architectural maps,* and *skeleton maps,* shown in the following illustrations. Consider these maps as suggestions; you can use any kind of map that physically details your network and best suits your needs.

The **schematic map** represents your network's arrangement of devices and cables, and is convenient for daily troubleshooting and maintenance. It does the following:

- identifies the type and function of each network device as well as its location in relation to the other network devices
- describes the connectivity between the devices (such as LocalTalk or Ethernet)
- describes the functions, memory capacity, and disk capacity for each network service and computer
- provides the names of network zones

Schematic map

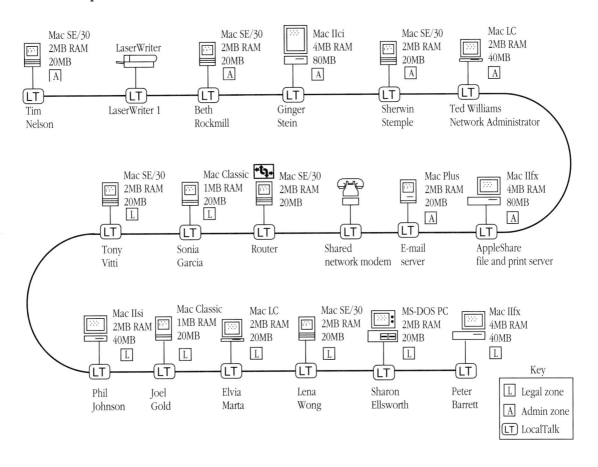

The **architectural map** shows the network's actual physical structure, including architectural elements such as stairways, walls, and windows. If you're administering a very small network, you can easily plan and troubleshoot using this map. However, as your network grows to include multiple floors and buildings, you'll find the schematic map much more manageable. (For small networks, you might also consider using a hybrid map that combines the components of the schematic and architectural maps.)

The architectural map is useful for planning the initial installation and for planning physical changes to the network, such as additions, relocation, or remodeling. It can provide people outside the company—such as support representatives or contractors—with a physical representation of the network and gives new users an idea of the network layout in the building or buildings. The components of an architectural map include:

- an area floor plan as close to scale as possible, including doors, windows, permanent walls, and cubicle walls
- potential architectural and electromagnetic obstructions that can affect cable and device installation, such as elevators, microwaves, and refrigerators
- device types and their locations within the building
- a scaled-down drawing of cable between devices

To create an architectural map, it's useful to obtain floor plans of your building to save time in measuring and drawing an original floor plan. Check with the facilities department of your company or the building management office of your building for a copy of the plan.

Architectural map

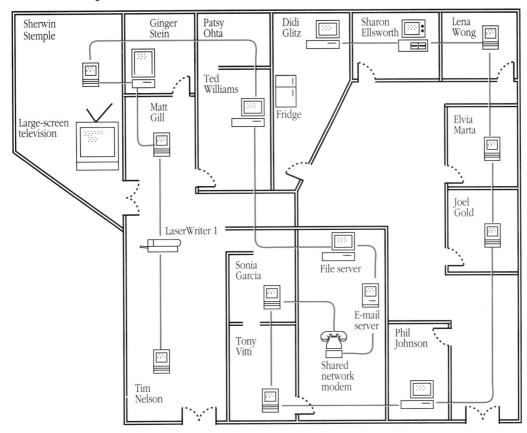

Skeleton maps are useful for visualizing interconnected networks in an internet and are best used in conjunction with schematic maps that detail each individual network. For reference purposes, it's helpful to label (and even color code) the different wiring schemes in your internet.

Skeleton map

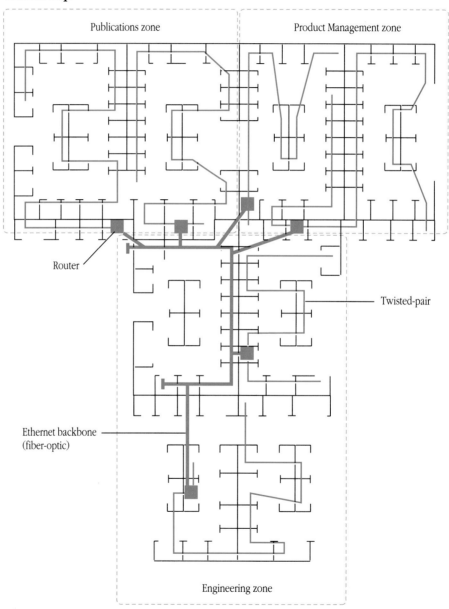

It's best to create your network map using a computer graphics application, such as MacDraw® II, or to use a network management application, such as NetAtlas (Farallon Computing) or GraceLAN (Technology Works), that automatically creates a map for you. If you simply draw the map on paper manually, then each future change in the layout will require you to erase and redraw the affected network segments. Unless your network is very small and simple, this may be difficult and time-consuming. Note that the Inter•Poll *Administration* disk includes symbols, such as icons for computers and LaserWriters, that can help you construct a network map.

Conclusion

Your main goal in designing your network is to create a balanced network that delivers an adequate level of performance and service to users. One of the most important considerations in network design centers around *network activity:* How many users will be on the network and what kinds of traffic will they generate? Once you have an idea of potential traffic activity, many design decisions—such as whether to have a single network or several connected networks—fall naturally into place.

As you design your network, also keep these general guidelines in mind:

- *Build the network slowly.* Avoid uncontrolled network growth by adding devices and software in an orderly way. Ask users to consult with you before doing anything that might affect the network. (Training users is a vital part of keeping the network running smoothly, and is discussed in Chapter 10.)

- *Avoid unnecessary through-traffic.* If users on one network require frequent access to users or devices on another network, be sure the networks are contiguous or linked by a backbone. Otherwise, any networks placed between them will be bogged down carrying constant through-traffic.

- *Control the assignment of device names, network numbers, and zone names.* These should be assigned by you and should be kept consistent to facilitate network monitoring and troubleshooting. In addition, try to give meaningful names to devices that will help users identify them, such as *2nd floor LaserWriter.*

- *Design your network with projected expansion in mind.* Assessing your current needs helps to define minimum requirements, but cannot produce a total design strategy. In your design plan, anticipate network expansion by projecting the increase in numbers of users and services, and in the anticipated level of network usage. By anticipating the way a network will evolve, you can help ensure that it will be easy to add new devices and to connect additional networks—while keeping communication between all points on the network as fast and efficient as possible.

8 Factors Affecting Installation

As you plan your network, it's important to consider the various factors that can affect network installation. This chapter focuses on the following general physical considerations:

- local building and fire codes

- electrical considerations, such as power system capacity

- sources of electromagnetic interference

- environmental conditions that may require special installation measures

- cable distribution and layout, including cable handling; labeling cables; and laying cable in a single room, multiroom, or multifloor site

Local building and fire codes

Building and fire codes differ in every county, so be sure to check local regulations before installing your network. For example, some local building codes require you to run cable through metal **conduit,** tubing which protects and insulates electrical wiring. Some local fire codes require that you use coated, fire-retardant **plenum cable** (such as LocalTalk Custom Cable) rather than **PVC cable,** which is not fire resistant and may emit toxic fumes if burned. Conduit or plenum cable is commonly required if cable passes between floors without being enclosed in a closet or power pole or if it passes through the ceiling in open spaces where flames can spread quickly. If you're using a contractor to install the cable, don't rely upon this person to know the codes in your area. Ultimately, your organization is responsible for ensuring that the network installation adheres to code.

Electrical considerations

The primary electrical consideration in installing a network is power system capacity. Verify that sufficient power is available for each device connected to the network and allow for adequate power for new devices as the network grows. Also check for power integrity. Power fluctuations can cause intermittent and hard-to-diagnose problems, including brownouts (extended voltage drops), blackouts, surges, and line interference. If power integrity is a problem in your building, consider installing an **uninterruptible power supply (UPS)** or a **constant voltage transformer (CVT).**

You should also check the electrical grounding of your installation to make sure that there is a common **earth ground** between all devices. Differences in the quality of the electrical ground between devices can result in a "ground loop"—external interference that can cause intermittent data transmission errors.

Electromagnetic interference

Avoid running cable near electrical or mechanical equipment, such as elevators, air conditioners, fluorescent lights, radio transmitters, and industrial machinery. Such equipment can cause electromagnetic interference, creating transmission disturbances that can potentially corrupt or destroy data. Cable should not be routed next to power lines unless the two are separated by conduit or a metal shield, as shown in the following figure.

When you are forced to run cables through large fields of interference, such as on a manufacturing floor with high-voltage electrical equipment, you may need to shield the cable with extra insulation or consider fiber-optic cable, which is immune to electromagnetic fields.

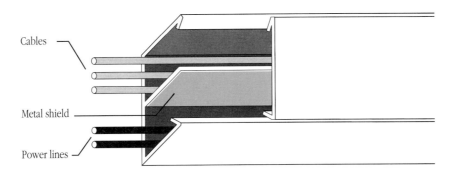

Cables

Metal shield

Power lines

Environmental factors

Ideally, your network should be maintained in a temperature-controlled area, free from excessive moisture and other adverse environmental conditions that can disturb the network's secure operation. If your network is subjected to unusual conditions such as high heat, caustic fumes, excessive dirt, moisture, or vibrations, you may need to take steps to provide protection for network equipment and cables. For example, a network that is located on a factory floor may have problems with excessive dust and debris that can clog equipment. If you need help in assessing or handling potential problems at your site, contact a professional network installer.

Cable distribution and layout

Planning cable layout carefully can save you a lot of time and money later on. Too often, cable installation is just an afterthought, and cable is strung haphazardly on walls and in exposed areas on the floor. This may be an easy way to lay cable, but it is also a potential source of transmission problems on the network. To protect the cable from physical abuse that can cause network failure, avoid laying cable across open floor areas, hallways, or in exposed areas where it can be easily stepped on. Route cable so that it is hidden and protected, yet is easily accessible and adaptable to new office arrangements.

Regardless of the cable distribution system you use, plan for repair, future modifications, and growth. The more accessible the cable is, the easier it will be to maintain or move. It makes sense to lay additional cable to accommodate new users on the network. If you run cable through **raceways** or conduits, plan them so they are large enough to accommodate extra cable for future expansion.

You also need to decide whether you (or someone in your organization) can perform the cable installation or whether you need to call in a professional to do some or all of the work. Most LocalTalk cable installations can be done quickly and easily without outside help. Occasionally, however, structural elements in some types of buildings make professional help desirable.

For other types of AppleTalk installations, such as PhoneNET, Token Ring, and some Ethernet networks, you'll probably need to enlist the help of outside professionals for cable layout. Such professionals include telephone installers, electrical contractors, or cable installation contractors. Even if you won't be doing the actual cable installation, being familiar with the procedures can be very helpful when talking with contractors and when troubleshooting network problems.

Handling cable

When you purchase cable, you'll receive information on how to handle it during installation. Improper cable handling can cause intermittent transmission problems on the network, making it difficult for you to locate the problem source. Before you install the cable, check its specifications for flexibility and bending. Some cable is more flexible than others; for instance, twisted-pair cable is more flexible than coaxial cable. When routing cable, try to make rounded bends rather than sharp ones that can kink the cable, causing damage and blocking transmission. A cable is not designed to support any weight—even its own. If you run cable without conduit or raceways, the cable should be secured with proper clamps along the route.

Attaching a cable to a wall improperly can produce such problems as kinking. For instance, if you run the cable through a metal staple attached to the wall, the staple can crimp the cable and kinking will result. If you need to attach cable to a wall, use the appropriate cable mounts. When pulling cable, especially through narrow openings, try not to exert excess force. Severe pulling can stretch or break the center conductor.

Labeling cables

It's good practice to label your network cables to avoid wiring confusion and to help in maintenance and troubleshooting. Labeling cables becomes especially important in installations where cable is hidden from view. Use some kind of logical numbering scheme so that you know where each cable comes from and where it goes. Putting the network number or network range on each cable is also a good idea. You may want to use color coding to differentiate cables further; for example, to denote different floors of a building. It's also a good idea to match your cable labels to your network map and to keep the map updated.

The label should be easy to read and long-lasting, but also easy to remove or change if necessary. Some stores sell self-sticking, preprinted numbered and colored labels, which saves time in creating your own.

Laying cable in a single room

If you're laying cable around a single large room in offices that have a flexible arrangement of devices, installation is very easy. You can simply string the cable along baseboards, preferably in a molding or raceway. Raceways are covered metal or plastic channels that can be attached to walls and installed around the edge of the room at baseboard or desktop height. Surface raceways are one of the simplest means for laying cable around a room. They protect the cable, are easy to maintain and modify, and eliminate the trouble and expense of going through walls, ceilings, or floors.

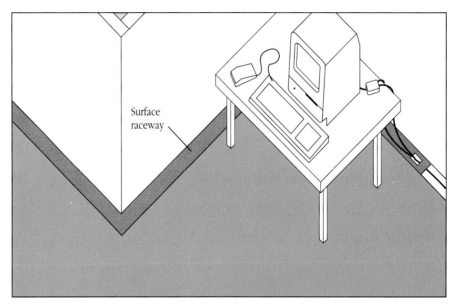

Surface raceway

Surface raceways around a single room

Laying cable in a multiroom or multifloor site

The design of most larger buildings includes a cable distribution system that accommodates communications and power lines between rooms and floors. Your building manager or facilities engineer should have a diagram of the system or be able to explain it to you.

The major types of cable distribution systems—ceiling systems, riser systems, and floor systems—are described in the following sections. To identify your type of multiroom or multistory installation, determine which of these general types of cable distribution systems is closest to your own building's arrangement.

Ceiling systems

One of the most flexible and economical ways to lay cable is through an accessible ceiling space, bringing cable down walls through power poles or raceways to the desired location. Ceiling distribution systems allow you to move cable easily and to keep cable lengths short.

In most code areas, cable in ceilings that carry used room air without air ducts (a **plenum air return**) must be insulated with flame-retardant materials or placed in conduit. The following figure shows a ceiling in which the used air is carried through air ducts (closed air returns) instead of through the entire ceiling space. If you have such a ceiling, some regulatory codes allow you to use non-flame-retardant PVC cable without conduit.

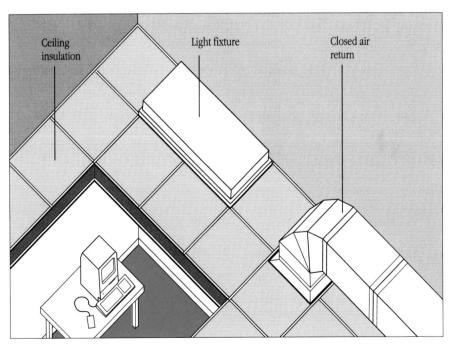

A ceiling system in which air is carried through ducts

Before you begin a ceiling installation, examine your ceiling for potential problems. Some older plaster ceilings may be inaccessible, and other ceilings may have inadequate clearance. The ceiling may also contain light fixtures, insulation, electrical boxes, air-conditioning systems, and antennas. If the clearance between such devices is less than three inches, laying the cable could be difficult. Some ceilings contain cable trays, racks, or hooks that are used to support large numbers of cables. If you are using such supports, leave at least one foot of clearance between unshielded power lines and cable to prevent radio-frequency interference.

A **ceiling grid system,** composed of prefabricated ducts to hold wiring, is often built into office buildings. Cables are laid through the ducts and brought into the office work spaces through power poles or raceways. You can access the grid system by temporarily removing strategic ceiling tiles.

A ceiling grid is one of the most flexible of all cable distribution systems. The following figure shows cable brought up through a utility pole and installed in a distribution duct for transport across the ceiling.

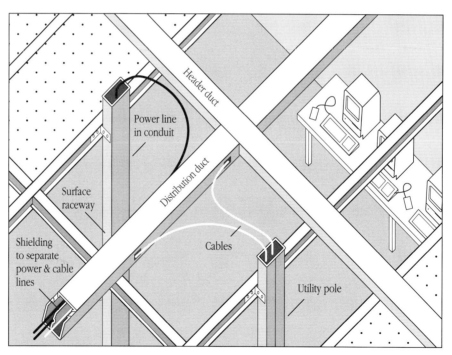

A ceiling grid system for routing cables

Remember, cable should not be installed directly next to unshielded power lines; instead, use a separate or divided duct. Most regulatory codes require you to use flame-retardant plenum cable in ceiling grids or to place PVC cable in conduit.

Riser systems

Riser systems are vertical structures extending from floor to floor through which utility lines can pass; these include shafts and wiring closets. Enclosed utility areas that are vertically aligned between floors are called **closed shaft systems.** The cable passes from a lower enclosure to one directly above through pipe or conduit embedded in the floor. **Open shafts** are areas where unenclosed cables pass from floor to floor. Strict codes are usually enforced for open shafts, and conduit or plenum cable is generally required.

If you're installing a multifloor network, you'll probably want to make use of centralized wiring closets that exist at your site. These wiring closets are typically installed for large-scale cable distribution. They provide a central point for incoming power and telephone lines and for data distribution between large central computers and office terminals. Because some AppleTalk networks are laid out in a linear topology, centralized wiring closets are not necessary, but they can be an excellent option if your wiring closets provide the major means of access from floor to floor. Wiring closets are typically used for star topology installations (such as unshielded twisted-pair LocalTalk networks and twisted-pair Ethernet networks) and are often used to run coaxial cable for Ethernet networks between floors.

Floor installation

Underfloor installation is another option for laying cable, either through underfloor ducts, cellular floors, or raised floors. An underfloor cable installation physically protects the cable and is quite secure from tampering, but may be impractical unless the cable is installed during building construction.

Underfloor duct systems are incorporated into the initial design of many large buildings. The ducts—prefabricated pipes in various sizes and cross-sectional pieces—are installed into the floor and provide protection and transport for cables.

As shown in the following figure, a duct system is usually composed of:

- *Header (or feeder) ducts.* These fit flush with the floor around its perimeter and may be covered with tile or carpet sections.
- *Distribution ducts.* These carry cables to various locations within the room.
- *Junction sites.* These provide access to header and distribution ducts.
- *Service fittings.* These are generally unmovable outlets under desks and along walls.

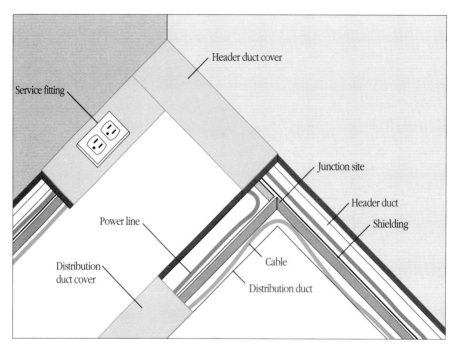

An underfloor duct system

Large-area ducts are used for communications wiring, small-area ducts for power lines. Some trenches may be partitioned with metal shielding so that communications lines and power lines can be installed together. Your existing ducts may already be at full capacity. To inspect them, remove the covers from ducts and junction boxes.

In **cellular floors,** the ducts and distribution cells that carry cables are intrinsic elements of the floor itself; that is, they perform two functions, architectural support and cable distribution. The distribution cells are usually steel or concrete and are fed by header ducts carrying cable from the wiring closets or shafts. The header ducts provide access to all cells in the floor.

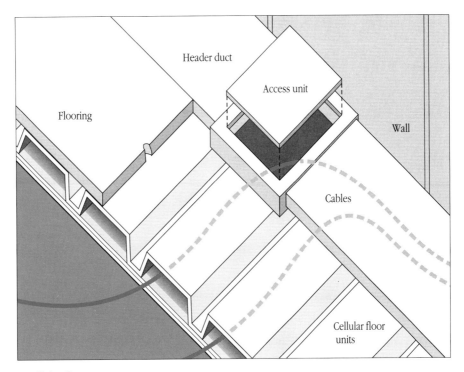

A cellular floor system

Since the cells are placed at close, regular intervals, cellular floors are more flexible than underfloor duct systems and can carry many more cables than a duct system can. As with other cable systems built into the structure of a building, careful planning at the time of construction is essential, because adding inserts after the floor is in place means drilling concrete. Remember to use separate or partitioned cells to avoid interference problems between unshielded power lines and cable.

A **raised floor,** commonly designed for large computers, is built over existing flooring and is made up of interlocking plates supported by metal standards, as shown in the following figure. The entire area under the floor is accessible, so cable installation is convenient and flexible. A disadvantage is that raised flooring is very expensive. When installing cables in a raised floor, be sure the floor is well grounded and be careful to warn others to stay away from any open grid areas. Some local building codes may require the use of conduit or flame-retardant cable in raised floors.

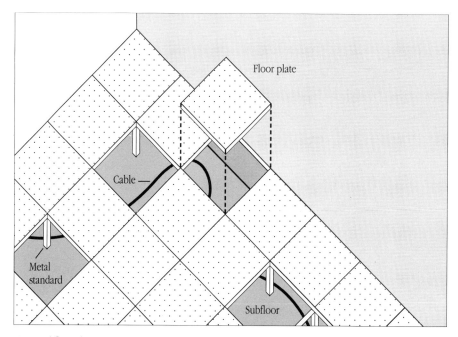

A raised floor design

Conclusion

This chapter has summarized some of the more general physical aspects to consider when installing your network. Obviously, network installation is a very broad topic and a great deal more can be said on the subject; however, such an expanded discussion is beyond the scope of this book. To learn more about installation issues, check the various networking books and journals in your local bookstore or library. Some specific references are listed below.

BOCA Basic/National Building Code, 1990 edition (with 1991 supplement). Produced by the Building Officials and Code Administrators (BOCA) International. 4051 Flossmoor Rd., Country Club Hills, IL 60478. (708) 799-2300.

Hands-On AppleTalk. Mike Rogers and Virginia Bare. Simon and Schuster. New York, New York. 1989.

Local Area Networks. John E. McNamara. Digital Press. Burlington, Massachusetts. 1985.

National Electrical Code (NEC). 1990 edition. Produced by the National Fire Protection Association. 1 Batterymarch Park, P.O. Box 9146, Quincy, MA 02269. (617) 770-3000.

Protection of Electronic Computer/Data Processing Equipment. 1989 edition. Produced by the National Fire Protection Association. 1 Batterymarch Park, P.O. Box 9146, Quincy, MA 02269. (617) 770-3000.

Standard Building Code (SBC), 1988 edition (1990 amendment). Produced by the Southern Building Code Congress International, Inc. 900 Montclair Rd., Birmingham, AL 35213. (205) 591-1853.

Uniform Building Code, 1991 edition. Produced by the International Conference of Building Officials (ICBO). 5360 S. Workman Mill Rd., Whittier, CA 90601. (213) 699-0541.

9 Security Considerations

An important part of planning your network is assessing your security needs. This chapter helps you define those needs and explore your security options, which include such simple measures as user education and password protection as well as more complex protection schemes such as data encryption.

Although network security is a relatively new area of focus for local area networks, it is also a rapidly growing one, and there are many products on the market today that can help you implement the security concepts discussed here.

Your network security needs

Security can be broadly defined as the process of protecting the data that is stored and transmitted on your network from unauthorized access, alteration, or destruction—whether from human error, malicious tampering, hardware malfunctioning, or environmental conditions. Security measures can take many forms, ranging from such basic measures as data backup and user education, to physical protection schemes, to sophisticated measures such as data encryption, which encodes network data.

The type of security you choose to implement will depend on the type of information transmitted and stored on your network, the scope or reach of your network, the physical environment in which the network is installed, and your budgetary requirements. You need to decide how critical or sensitive the information on your network is, where the potential risks are, and what kinds of security protection make the most sense for you.

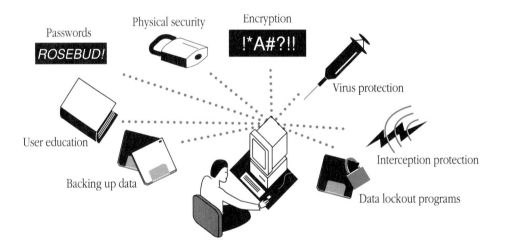

When assessing your security needs, evaluate how your organization would be affected if the information on your network were lost, stolen, or damaged. If your network is small and the data is not highly confidential or critical, then simple security measures are probably sufficient. But the larger and more complex the network is, and the more critical the data on the network is, the greater the security issues will be. For instance, if the information on your network consists of routine office data, security concerns might center around accidental misuse rather than malice, and user education and backup procedures may be sufficient. However, if your network contains highly confidential data—such as personnel information, electronic funds, or product development plans—then more stringent security measures such as data encryption and perhaps even network isolation (a completely separate network) may be necessary.

A key point to keep in mind: *be realistic when considering your security needs.* Although establishing adequate security is essential, establishing more security than is necessary is costly, inconvenient, and time-consuming. Consider the repercussions of unauthorized data access and data loss, weigh this against the inconvenience or cost imposed by the security measure, and then decide what type of security best meets the needs of your network.

Backing up data

Backing up shared data on file servers and mail servers is an essential part of network security, since it may be your only way to recover information that has been destroyed, lost, or tampered with in some way. The responsibility for backing up data is often one of the most vital aspects of an administrator's job.

If the information you are backing up is confidential, make sure the backup tapes or disks are locked in a secure location. For especially critical information, multiple backup copies should be kept at different, secure locations, including one off-site location. This way, even if your site experienced an environmental catastrophe, your data would still be safe. Backup methods and media are discussed fully in Chapter 10.

Educating users about security

One of the most basic and important elements in a network security plan is sometimes the most overlooked: the *people* who will be using the network. The best-planned network security may never work if users don't understand or aren't committed to using established security procedures. Your organization can start educating users by establishing formal policies on security measures. If users understand why such measures are needed, they are usually happy to comply, making your job much easier. Without such user acceptance, you may be continually frustrated in your security efforts.

As the network administrator, it's important to define your security role and to communicate this role to users. Decide how much control you need to have over security and how much can be entrusted to others in the organization. Part of your job is to make users aware of security measures (or remind them of stated company policies) and to help users better understand why they're necessary.

For instance, if the integrity of your network information depends on password protection, explain to users that they shouldn't write a script or macro that will automatically log a computer on to a server, because it bypasses the normal log-on process—negating the password protection you have established. Let users know that they should log off a network service when they leave their computers so that someone else can't access the service (and possibly penetrate the network further) while they're gone.

You may need to make it clear to users why they can't just add a piece of equipment to the network without your knowledge. For instance, if your network is a high-security installation where remote access is not allowed, users need to understand that they can't add a modem to the network to access their computers from home because the modem may create an entry point for unauthorized users.

It's important to train network users so that they have a basic understanding of network functions, components, and procedures. This training will help to prevent accidental misuse of equipment or software. For example, users need to know that the Macintosh computer sitting outside their offices is a router, *not* a workstation. They should understand what each piece of equipment is and how it works, and that they shouldn't tamper with servers and routers unless they have your OK.

Training will also help users understand the reasoning behind certain security measures. If users understand that a security breach compromises data on their own computers as well as on *connected* computers and servers with confidential information, they are more likely to adopt security practices.

It's the responsibility of your organization not only to establish security measures, but to enforce them as well. It's a good idea to give employees incentives so that security is an essential part of their jobs. Consider having periodic security reviews to help ensure that procedures are being followed and to make it clear that security is a high-priority area. The bottom line? Security is an organizational commitment and is literally *everyone's* business.

Physical security

There are a variety of physical security measures you can use to protect your data and equipment. If your network is vulnerable to physical intrusion (for example, in a public setting where many people have easy access to your network), then your data may be at risk in spite of other measures you take. After all, even the best password protection scheme won't help if someone runs off with your disks or file server.

Equipment can be physically secured in a variety of ways. Servers and routers can be placed in locked rooms or in cabinets with adequate ventilation. Tapes and disks (including backups) that contain sensitive information can be locked up. There are also physical locking mechanisms that can be installed on computers to prevent access to the disk drives or power switch. Computers, servers, and routers can also be physically locked down by anchoring them with padlocks and cables or security pads.

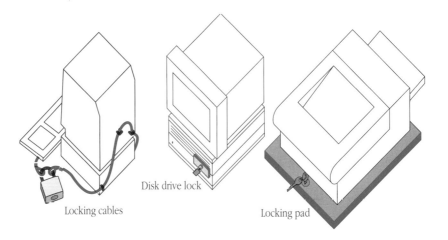

Locking cables

Disk drive lock

Locking pad

Other physical controls include removing monitors and keyboards from servers (commonly called *headless servers*); placing cables out of sight and, if possible, in protective raceways to avoid accidental misuse (such as cables being stepped on), cable tapping, or penetration by monitoring devices; and placing network printers that are used to print confidential information in locked rooms or in supervised areas that are off limits to unauthorized users.

Finally, if part of your organization transmits or stores data of a highly sensitive nature, your best choice may be to isolate those users in their own separate network, providing them with their own file servers, mail servers, printers, and so on.

Controlling access to data

An integral part of any network security scheme is the ability to restrict access to information. Files stored on a user's computer can be protected with special security software. Network services, such as file service, electronic mail, and remote access should identify authorized users with an ID and a password. File service should provide the capability to restrict access to information and to specify what kind of access users can have, such as read or write access.

Using passwords

The password protection in AppleShare and in other network services, such as electronic mail and remote access, is a good deterrent to unauthorized access if used properly. However, passwords are often treated casually and can be a vulnerable weak spot in a security system. To use password protection effectively, follow the guidelines below and explain appropriate information to network users.

- *Make passwords hard to guess.* Don't use such easily broken "codes" as first or last names; the names of children, pets, or spouses; social security numbers; birthdates; or initials. This kind of information can be easily obtained by someone seriously motivated to access the system. Instead, choose a long string of random characters with spaces, numbers, and letters (mix upper and lower case). One technique for generating passwords that are seemingly random but easy to remember is to make up a nonsense sentence and use the first letter (or number) of each word to compose the password. For example, "This morning 7 cows and 3 geese sang," would yield the password "Tm7c+3gs."

- *Change passwords frequently (but make sure you remember them!).* This way, even if someone learns your password, it won't be useful to the person for very long. If password security is important to your organization, you may choose to take control of creating and distributing passwords by changing users' passwords automatically on a regular basis (but let them know this routine and why you're doing it). Alternatively, you can require users to change their own passwords regularly.

- *Keep passwords strictly confidential.* Users should memorize their passwords. They should not share passwords with coworkers unless absolutely necessary and they should avoid jotting down passwords and leaving them where they can be discovered by someone else. Keep any administrator passwords memorized or in a secure, locked location. Anyone who has access to an AppleShare file server and who knows the administrator's password can obtain confidential information on the server.

- *When an employee leaves the company, remove that person's password or account immediately.* This ensures that neither the ex-employee or someone that person knows can use the password to access the network.

- *Avoid scripts or macros that automatically provide user passwords.* The ability to log on automatically can provide unauthorized users with easy entry into a network.

Protecting information on workstations

To protect data on workstations, users have several options. One option is to store all sensitive files on floppy disks, locking the disks up at the end of each day. Another choice is to install a **data lockout program** on the computer. These programs protect folders and files by requiring a password (either at startup or when someone tries to access the folder or file) or by creating password-protected "safes" that lock data inside. Some programs enable users to activate the lockout process at any time, a convenient feature that prevents intruders from accessing unattended computers during the course of the day. A third option for protecting files is to use software that enables you to **encrypt** or code data files.

Data encryption is a high-end security measure that can go a long way towards protecting sensitive files on the network. Encryption is the process of changing intelligible data into unintelligible data. A password, called a **key,** is used to encrypt and decrypt files. When a file is encrypted, only those who know the key can read it. Even if an unauthorized person manages to gain access to an encrypted file, that person will not be able to make any sense of it without the key.

Some data encryption products are used strictly to protect files stored on disk. Other products also enable you to transmit an encrypted file over the network or copy the encrypted file onto other media, such as floppy disks or tape. Be aware that if a product does not have the capability to transmit encrypted files over the network, then any encrypted files you transmit (through electronic mail, for example) can be potentially intercepted and read.

Encrypted files are unreadable unless you have the password.

There are a wide range of encryption processes available, from simple encryption that protects against the accidental or "casual abuser" to sophisticated methods that protect against all but the most highly trained criminal with an in-depth knowledge of cryptanalysis, the analysis and deciphering of codes.

Rigorous encryption methods are based on mathematical algorithms that make it very difficult for even mainframe computers to break the code. The National Bureau of Standards has established its own Data Encryption Standard (DES), which is recommended for extremely sensitive applications such as electronic financial transactions. Some encryption products use their own algorithms; others have adopted DES as their basis for encryption. Before purchasing encryption software, make sure that the encryption technique is reliable and that you understand how the vendor handles selection and distribution of encryption keys. Once the data is encrypted, it is useless to unauthorized users, but if the encryption key is compromised (or forgotten!), the process is useless to you as well.

◆ **Note** To send encrypted files or encryption software outside of the United States, you may need approval from the Defense Trade Center (National Security Agency) in Washington D.C. Call (703) 875-6644 for details. ◆

Protecting information on file servers

If you need strict control over access to shared data, you may want to consider using a centralized file service, such as AppleShare, where control ultimately resides with one person—the network administrator. A centralized file service also enables you to place the server in a physically secure location, such as a locked room or cabinet. If you store confidential information in a distributed file-sharing environment, individual users must be well aware of security measures and take any necessary precautions to protect data.

As discussed in Chapter 3, an AFP file server has built-in security mechanisms to safeguard information. For example, with AppleShare you can control file access at the file server level and at the folder level. Users can also protect their own folders without the administrator's intervention.

Security provisions at the file server level include user name and password log-on (encrypted password) and restricted access to file server volumes. AppleShare also allows you to create private volumes that permit access by designated users only. It's especially critical to keep the administrator password, which allows access to all folders stored on a server, confidential.

You can restrict access to folders in several ways. You can permit folder access by specified users only, hide folders from unauthorized users, and specify further whether users can just view or make changes to a folder. AppleShare also enables you to lock folders to prevent them from being deleted, moved, or renamed. AppleShare's "drop folder" security feature is like a private mailbox, enabling users to put files into a folder that only the owner of the folder can see and retrieve.

If you're using Novell NetWare 2.15 or a Digital VAX as a file server, you can take advantage of the added security features built into those systems. NetWare enables you to implement stringent security controls (including enforced password requirements, audit trails, and restricted log-on attempts) to prevent unauthorized access to server resources. Using a Digital VAX as a file server allows you to take advantage of the full range of VAX/VMS security mechanisms. This includes extensive mechanisms to control access to the system and the data stored on it, and to monitor activity to ensure that access is restricted to authorized users. The VAX also has automated backup features, which is especially convenient for networks that store large amounts of data on the server.

One final point about making file service more secure: encourage users to log off a network service when they leave their computers—even if it's just for a few minutes. This not only prevents unauthorized users from accessing the service, it also prevents others from reading information left on the screen that they should not see.

◆ **Note** If you want to store encrypted files on a file server, be aware that some encryption products do not protect files transmitted over the network (from the server to individual computers). The safest procedure is to encrypt the file locally (the data and application should be on your local hard disk), then copy the encrypted file to the server. When you need to access the encrypted file, copy the file to your hard disk, then run the application locally to decrypt the file. ◆

Remote-access concerns

Remote access (discussed in Chapter 3) is a valuable productivity tool, allowing users to access the resources of the network from a remote location over modems and phone lines. However, because remote access is a hook into your network and can be a potential source of intrusion by unauthorized users, it's wise to take precautions to safeguard this access.

Remote access can be made more secure by using a remote-access product that provides user name and password validation, call auditing, or automatic *callback* procedures. With callback security, instead of directly accessing a computer or peripheral device, users call another device (such as a server or modem) and enter a user ID and a password. The device then disconnects the call, confirms the ID and password information, and calls the user back using the preset telephone number associated with that password, enabling the user to connect to the network. The security features may be built into a modem (security modems) or they may be part of the remote-access software.

A note of caution: if the data on your network is very sensitive, you may want to eliminate or at least strictly regulate remote access.

Preventing interception of network signals

Any time information is transmitted through a computer cable, monitor, or printer, that information can potentially be intercepted in the form of electromagnetic impulses (EMI) or radio-frequency signals. These signals can be picked up by monitoring devices, recorded, and then interpreted. Sophisticated devices can intercept transmission signals a considerable distance away from the source.

If you have a network that requires stringent security control, you might want to consider some of the following precautions to protect the network from EMI interception:

- Place cables out of sight and in protective conduit to discourage physical cable tapping.
- Add additional shielding to your cable to reduce EMI leakage.

- Use fiber-optic cable, which eliminates EMI emission problems entirely, since light pulses are used in place of electronic signals.

- Use an electromagnetic field emitter, an inexpensive device that emits a jamming signal to thwart attempts to steal EMI emissions.

- Keep equipment away from exterior windows. It would be difficult to pick up transmission signals without a clear view of the equipment.

- Install shielding devices on computers that reduce or eliminate EMI emanations.

Computer viruses

A discussion of network security would not be complete without a few words on **computer viruses.** A virus is a computer program that is added to otherwise harmless software and is capable of replicating itself and spreading to other computers. It can infect a system without causing great harm—by displaying a message, for example—cause strange occurrences such as hiding files or making an application suddenly quit, or it can be programmed to do great damage—such as corrupting files or erasing a hard disk. Computer viruses are not new; they have been around almost as long as computers have. But what *is* new is the number of people who use viruses as an opportunity to test their imaginations and computer penetration skills or, perhaps even worse, as a means of sabotage.

Viruses are introduced into a computer or network by adding software that has been infected with a viral code. This software can come from a variety of sources—file servers, bulletin board services, purchased software, shareware, and so forth. Control panels and system extensions can also be infected with viruses (in Macintosh system software prior to System 7, control panels are referred to as Control Panel device packages, or CDEVs, and system extensions are called INIT files).

In general, viruses can spread from one application to other applications, attack specific files, occupy disk space and memory, and damage files that use infected applications. File servers are often the most common source of workgroup infections, because so many people share information on the server. In fact, computers connected to a server can be infected just by running an infected application that resides on the server.

You can help prevent a virus from infecting your network (or recover quickly from an infection) by following some simple guidelines:

- *Write-protect all master floppy disks to prevent a virus from attaching to your originals.* Write-protecting locks a disk so that no changes can be made to its contents, preventing viral infections. Master copies of all applications should be stored on write-protected disks and locked up for maximum security.

- *Test all new applications and files (particularly questionable public domain software) with a virus-detection program before they are used or loaded on a hard disk or added to a file server's volumes.* There are a number of commercially available programs that can prevent, diagnose, and eliminate many known viruses. Such programs can analyze the contents of a disk and supply detailed information on what specific applications, if any, have been infected. Some will also continually scan for symptoms typical of viruses and alert you to potential problems (some system extensions, or INITs, can do this).

  Before using a new application or file or loading it on a hard disk, run the virus-detection program to check for infection. Make sure you install upgrades of the program as new versions become available that detect newly discovered viruses.

  You may want to consider setting up a "virus-checking station"—a computer not connected to any network that just runs a virus-detection program from a locked floppy disk. This will make it easier for users to check their floppy disks (and, if virus-detection procedures are easy, they will be more inclined to use them). In addition, you may want to recommend that users set up an automatic virus-detection program on each of their computers.

- *Know the source and integrity of all software installed on computers, especially if it's being placed on a file server.* Use master copies of commercially available software whenever possible. If you want to use software from other sources, stick with reputable sources. For instance, copying software from an obscure bulletin board service that doesn't monitor postings for viruses will obviously be more of a risk than a reputable service that does. Your best bet: always check new applications with a virus-detection program.

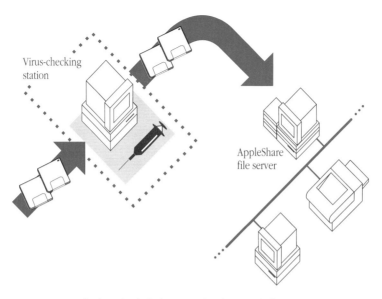

Virus-checking
station

AppleShare
file server

- *Run regularly scheduled virus checks on all file servers.* The earlier you detect an infected server, the fewer the number of computers that will be infected.

- *Regularly back up all important information.* Using backup copies may be your only recourse if a virus has seriously infected a computer. Make duplicates of all applications, files, utilities, desk accessories, and system files that you consider difficult to replace. Keep backups from different time periods and do not continuously copy over the same backup. This prevents you from unknowingly transferring a virus to your most recent backup. Users should follow a set schedule (daily or weekly) for backing up.

- *Educate users about viruses.* Educate users about the dangers of using unauthorized applications and files, loading unchecked applications onto their hard drives, placing applications on the file server without your OK, and neglecting to back up files on a regular basis. Encourage them to use virus-detection programs regularly.

When do you suspect that a computer might have a virus? When a computer begins to do things out of the ordinary or when it stops being able to do things it has always done in the past and *normal troubleshooting techniques have failed to correct the problem,* it's time to investigate the possibility of a virus.

When you do detect a virus or strongly suspect that you have one, disconnect the infected computer from the network immediately to keep the virus from spreading. Then follow these steps to eliminate it:

- If the virus-detection program you're using has an eradication capability, use it.
- If you can identify the corrupted file, delete it.
- If the infected file is *invisible,* perform a file-by-file backup of the disk, then reinitialize the disk and restore each file. Only the visible files will be backed up and restored, eliminating the infected file.
- If the previous three steps don't eliminate the virus, reinitialize the hard drive and restore the data from master copies and backups.

In summary, although viruses *are* a threat in today's computer networks, you can take solid measures to protect your network. Follow the guidelines discussed here, take immediate action if a virus does attack your network, and educate users thoroughly.

Conclusion

Computer networks have made it easy for people to exchange and share information—down the hall or across the continent. And yet this same ease of access has opened the door for a variety of threats to data security. Those responsible for protecting the security of an organization's valuable information—including network administrators—often find themselves in the middle of this situation, trying to balance the need for security against the obvious productivity advantages gained through easy network access and use. Fortunately, these seemingly opposing goals can both be satisfied. By taking a middle-ground approach and establishing a reasonable level of security, you'll be able to handle this balancing act, keeping your data secure without placing undue restrictions on users.

Part 3 Managing Your Network

Once the network is up and running, you'll need to spend time managing the network to ensure that it functions as smoothly as possible. The amount of time you spend depends on a number of factors, such as the size and complexity of your network and how dynamic your network environment is. Network management can be divided into three key areas: monitoring, maintenance, and troubleshooting.

Monitoring is a kind of preventive medicine for your network. By checking the network on a routine basis, you can discover potential problems before they interfere with user needs. Using traffic-monitoring tools, you can gauge the level and nature of network activity, heading off potential bottlenecks that can cause slowdowns in network services. By checking the integrity of network connections, you can uncover breaks that could significantly disrupt communication. As a network grows, monitoring becomes especially important to maintain network integrity and an acceptable level of performance.

Network maintenance covers a wide variety of day-to-day administrative tasks that keep the network running efficiently. You'll upgrade system software, add users to the network, and back up shared files on network servers. You'll keep records of your own activities in a logbook, train users, keep the servers organized, and make sure that licensing agreements are not violated.

Troubleshooting involves step-by-step procedures—not to mention a healthy bit of detective work—to track down and remedy network problems. If a user inadvertently disconnects a segment of the cable, it's up to you to discover and solve the problem. If network performance slows down as the result of some mysterious cause, you must locate and correct the situation.

The ultimate goal of all network management is providing network users with the highest possible network performance—with the fewest possible disruptions in their network services. The final chapters of this book provide guidelines and strategies to help you achieve this goal.

10 Network Maintenance Guidelines

There are many tasks an administrator performs to keep the network operating smoothly. Some of these tasks fall into the monitoring category, and involve routine checks of the network to detect problems before they cause disruptions in network services. Other tasks performed by the administrator are of a general maintenance nature, such as training users and backing up shared files.

This chapter discusses the basics of maintaining your network, providing information on

- keeping network logbooks and generating network reports

- using administrative tools to monitor network activity

- backing up and restoring shared files, with details about different kinds of backups, backup media, and backup schedules

- supporting and training users

- upgrading system software

- adding users and services

- managing servers

- optimizing network performance

Keeping logbooks

Aside from the network map, a network **logbook** is one of the most indispensable records you can keep. A logbook provides a historical record of network activity and serves as a reference for monitoring and troubleshooting your network. For example, when a problem arises, your logbook can help you identify any significant network change that took place at roughly the same time the problem began. A logbook is especially useful in situations where more than one person administers the network, since it enables the backup administrator to stay up-to-date on what's been happening.

Every network will have a different logging system based on its specific requirements. However, all networks should begin with the *Network Activity Log* to record basic network activity, shown below.

		NETWORK ACTIVITY LOG		
Date	Time	Admin's. Initials	Activities Performed	Admin's. Time
5/8	8:00 am	SG	Made physical connection for a 16 node LocalTalk network and installed LaserWriter drivers to create new network.	5 hrs.
6/5	10:00 am	SG	Installed AppleShare File Server on Macintosh II in supply room to allow for shared files. Created 16 users and 16 folders.	1.5 hrs.
6/6	1:00 pm	JZ	Created group folders for Administration, Support, Publications, and Art on NoName Server, Gold Server volume. Used for group projects and time sheets.	5 hr

You may opt for a format such as this one or create your own. For a small network, this one log might suffice. For larger networks, additional logbooks may be necessary to record such information as the dates and times of data backup, network service activity, and equipment purchases. Establish a logbook as soon as your network is operational, and keep it updated. Whatever the size of your network, start with a simple logging system—one that's easily manageable—and add to it as needs arise.

There's no recipe for a logbook that will work for everyone. Consider the way your network is used and the way your own time is spent so you can design a format tailored to meet your network's needs. The basic Network Activity Logbook should record

- who performed the activity
- what was specifically done
- where the activity took place
- when the activity took place
- why the activity took place

Beyond these "five W's" of good logbook entries, you need to know whether the time you spend as network administrator should be recorded in your logbook. Is network administration your sole job in the company or do you perform other functions as well? If your management wants you to record the hours you spend performing administrator functions, this is an ideal place to do it. Another factor to consider when designing your logbook is the amount of experience you have as a network administrator. If this is a new job for you, or if an AppleTalk network is new to you, it's important to make detailed notes in your logbook for every network activity you perform. These records will be invaluable to you if problems occur.

After you've established the Network Activity Log, determine what other logs or additional sections to the Network Activity Log you need to create. Ask your company managers what information they need. Ask yourself what kinds of records you might want to keep about network activities and services. If you're responsible for keeping track of equipment purchases or service contracts, you may need to keep a Network Equipment Log or folder. Here you can organize receipts, pricing and warranty information, service contracts, and serial numbers. If you're responsible for tracking supplies, such as printer paper and toner cartridges, you can keep a Network Supplies Log. Other useful logbooks include the Network Backup Log, the Network Service Log, and the Users and Groups Log.

Recording accurate backup information is essential. If your network is small and backups are performed infrequently, then you can probably record this information in the Network Activity Log. However, if your network is large and backups are performed frequently, it's a good idea to create a Network Backup Log strictly for recording backup activity.

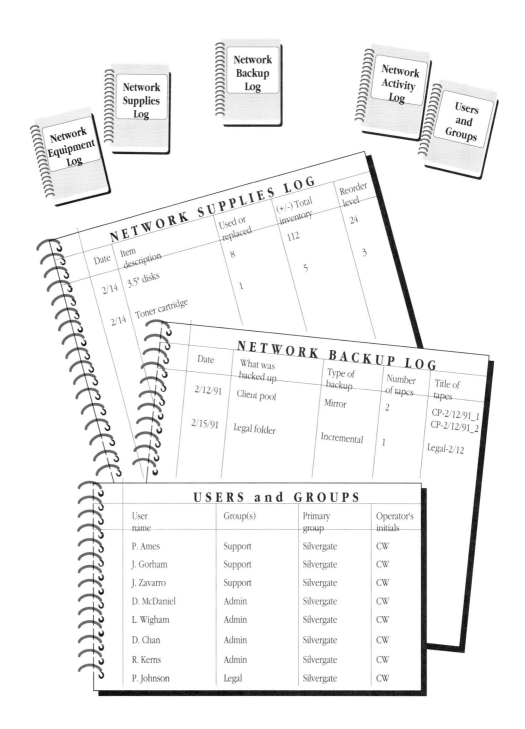

NETWORK SUPPLIES LOG

Date	Item description	Used or replaced	(+/-) Total inventory	Reorder level
2/14	3.5" disks	8	112	24
2/14	Toner cartridge	1	5	3

NETWORK BACKUP LOG

Date	What was backed up	Type of backup	Number of tapes	Title of tapes
2/12/91	Client pool	Mirror	2	CP-2/12/91_1 CP-2/12/91_2
2/15/91	Legal folder	Incremental	1	Legal-2/12

USERS and GROUPS

User name	Group(s)	Primary group	Operator's initials
P. Ames	Support	Silvergate	CW
J. Gorham	Support	Silvergate	CW
J. Zavarro	Support	Silvergate	CW
D. McDaniel	Admin	Silvergate	CW
L. Wigham	Admin	Silvergate	CW
D. Chan	Admin	Silvergate	CW
R. Kerns	Admin	Silvergate	CW
P. Johnson	Legal	Silvergate	CW

Similarly, network size is an important factor in deciding whether you need a separate Network Service Logbook. How many file servers does your network have and how many volumes are there per server? How many printers do you have? Do you have E-mail? A Network Service Log can help you track the overall activity on the network as well as your most frequent users and the specific services and volumes they access. This information will be useful when you're planning network service upgrades and expansion.

You may want to consider a Users and Groups Log if the network service software you use does not provide a way to record this information or if you have many users within a variety of groups. This logbook will help you keep track of user names, the primary groups to which they belong, and the volumes and files they can access.

If you have an internet, it's a good idea to keep a logbook or a section of your logbook for recording network numbers and ranges, zone names, and zone lists. If your router software provides a way to record this information, a written record can also serve as a backup copy.

The administrator's primary monitoring tools

There are a variety of software packages that can help you manage the network from your own computer. Network management software can help you do the following:

- *Identify missing devices.* By displaying lists of active devices, zones, and internets, you can pinpoint network problems. If devices that should be active do not appear on the list, there may be a break in the network.

- *Gather system software information and a multitude of other information about the computers on the network.* Various software packages report such information as system software versions, Finder™ or MultiFinder® versions, memory size, system extensions (INITs), and desk accessories. The ability to check this information from your own computer saves a great deal of administrative time.

- *Test the integrity and response time of network connections and devices.* These tests are useful for identifying such network problems as faulty cables, improperly terminated cables, excessive traffic, or other transmission problems.

- *Monitor traffic activity on a network.* You can identify sources of network traffic, measure the quantity of traffic, and create a variety of graphs to help you quickly analyze traffic patterns.

- *Monitor traffic activity and errors across a router.* If you have an internet, it's important to monitor this activity, since excessive traffic across a router can impede network performance.

- *Access devices remotely and run network administration programs.* This can be invaluable for solving users' problems and administering network services.

These administrative tools have a dual identity: as monitoring tools and, if problems do arise, as troubleshooting tools. Chapter 11 discusses how to use these tools for specific troubleshooting strategies.

When you first begin using administrative tools to detect errors and monitor traffic, the results may not have immediate significance to you. Over time, however, you'll become familiar with normal levels of errors and activity and will quickly learn to interpret deviations that could signal potential network problems.

The following sections discuss each of these network management capabilities.

Identifying missing devices

Device lists that display all of the active devices on the network—those that are connected and turned on—are very helpful for monitoring the network and for pinpointing network problems. It's important to print a device list when your network is first established and then any time you add or remove a network device. Keep these lists in your logbook for later reference and comparison when troubleshooting.

If network devices that should be on the device list do not show up, there could be a break in the network. By comparing the device list with your reference device list or network map, you can find out which devices are missing. The network map can help you identify the exact location of a network break.

An example device list produced by Apple's Inter•Poll software is shown in the following figure. As you can see from this example, the device list includes computers as well as shared devices such as servers and printers. The list also displays the number of the network on which the device is connected, the name of the registered user for each active device, and the zone to which each device belongs.

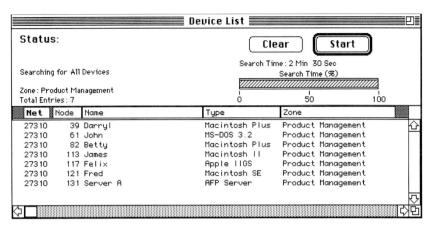

A sample Inter•Poll device list

Identifying system versions and other information

You can also use network management software to display a wide variety of information about the computers on your network, enabling you to gather information without leaving your desk. Depending on the software package, you'll be able to check such information as system software versions, Finder or MultiFinder versions, AppleShare versions, memory size, the types of NuBus™ cards installed, SCSI devices connected, system extensions (INITs), fonts, and desk accessories.

As shown in the following figure, Inter•Poll enables you to list the versions of the System file, Finder file, and LaserWriter driver for Macintosh computers that have the *Responder* file installed. Conflicting versions of system software files can be a common source of network problems. Different LaserWriter driver versions, for example, may reinitialize the printer, causing long delays in printing. The ability to check system versions quickly from your own computer is very convenient when troubleshooting.

```
≣□■≣≣≣≣≣≣≣≣≣≣≣≣≣≣ System Information ≣≣≣≣≣≣≣□■≣

Display:   ● System File Version              ┌─────────────────────┐
           ○ Finder File Version              │   Get System Info   │
                                              └─────────────────────┘
           ○ LaserWriter Driver Version

Name              Type            System File Version
Morton, Ron       Macintosh IIci  Macintosh System version 6.0.7⊚ Apple C…  ⬆
Gary Henry's Ma…  Macintosh IIci  Macintosh System File Version 7.0, ⊚ Ap…  ▊
Regello, Carolyn  Macintosh II    Macintosh System File Version 7.0, ⊚ Ap…
Kerns, Robin      Macintosh II    Macintosh System File version 6.0.5⊚ 19…
Patrick Ames      Macintosh II    Macintosh System File Version 7.0, ⊚ Ap…
<Unnamed>-1       Macintosh II    Macintosh System File Version 7.0, ⊚ Ap…
Clark, Charlotte  Macintosh IIci  Macintosh System version 6.0.7⊚ Apple C…
<Unnamed>         Macintosh II    Macintosh System File Version 7.0, ⊚ Ap…
Grant, Patrice    Macintosh IIx   Macintosh System File Version 7.0, ⊚ Ap…
Della Gallion     Macintosh II    Macintosh System File version 6.0.5⊚ 19…
Oates, Michael    Macintosh IIci  Macintosh System File Version 7.0, ⊚ Ap…
Reece, Becky      Macintosh II    Macintosh System File  Version 6.0.2Cop…
Administrator     Macintosh II    Macintosh System File Version 7.0, ⊚ Ap…
René              Macintosh II    Macintosh System File version 6.0.5⊚ 19…  ⬇
GREENE, LISA      Macintosh II    Macintosh System File Version 7.0, ⊚ Ap…
Soule, Tom        Macintosh II    Macintosh System File version 6.0.5⊚ 19…  ↳
```

Checking system software versions with Inter•Poll

Testing network integrity

Administrative software tools are also helpful for testing the integrity of network connections and transmissions. One such network test is called a **loopback test,** which enables you to send test packets to a device to check for problems in the transmission path. Loopback tests can help you check network connections and potential traffic congestion. For example, Inter•Poll enables you to send echo and printer packets to test link integrity between the computer running Inter•Poll and any active named device (shown in the following figure).

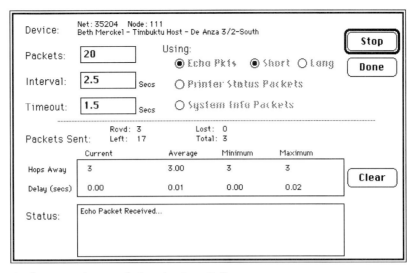

Sending test packets to a device using Inter•Poll

Other software tests provide statistics on a variety of network errors:

- *timeout errors,* which are caused by packet collisions on a network. They may indicate a problem with the device sending the packets.

- *overrun errors,* which result when the administrator's computer cannot keep up with the traffic it is receiving, and data is subsequently lost

- *CRC (cyclic redundancy check) errors,* which indicate that a packet has been received damaged during transmission. This may be caused by cable problems or by excessive network traffic.

- *length errors,* which typically indicate a software problem at the sending device

Error statistics can reveal a great deal about the health of your network. Although it's common for a network to have some errors, a large number of errors may indicate a problem. For example, if errors increase during peak traffic hours, you may need to segment your network by installing a bridge or router.

You can also check for network reliability and for errors that occur during routing from one network to the next. For example, the AppleTalk Internet Router software displays the percentage of total packets routed without error. During peak traffic periods, network reliability may drop slightly, but an efficient network typically operates above a 98% reliability level. Router software can also provide you with a host of other error statistics to keep you informed about the router's operation.

⊛ File Edit View Special Router				
Port Statistics for Router: CC3-7th/South				
Packets Routed:	10,361,936		Network Reliability:	98.1%
Recent Activity Rate:	Idle ▮▯▯▯▯▯▯▯▯ Busy		Recent Network Error Rate:	Low ▯▯▯▯▯▯▯▯▯ High
Statistics last reset at: Wed, Mar 6, 1991 1:58 PM				

Statistic	Total	EtherTalk Slot 3	LocalTalk Printer	LocalTalk Phone
Packets In	9910495	4758918	1797996	3353581
Packets Out	9909000	5507972	1960393	2440635
Name Requests In	169323	147706	17083	4534
Name LookUps Out	452936	408018	22459	22459
Data Link Errors	23922	151	10186	13585
Packet Buffer Overflow	186023	11314	6101	168608
Unknown Network	1495	1373	52	70
Hop Count Exceeded	0	0	0	0
Routing Table Overflow	0	0	0	0
Local Net Setup Conflicts	0	0	0	0
Remote Net Range Conflicts	0	0	0	0
Router Version Mismatch	0	0	0	0

Monitoring traffic activity

You may find it useful to include a traffic-monitoring tool, such as TrafficWatch (from Farallon Computing), in your administrative arsenal. Such a software tool can help you identify

- which devices are generating traffic
- how much traffic is being generated
- when traffic is occurring during the day

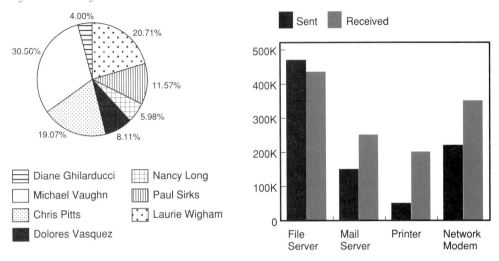

A tool such as TrafficWatch can help you analyze traffic patterns. For example, you can see how much traffic is generated by each user or by each device.

It's a good idea to gather representative traffic data on a routine basis to help optimize network performance over time. For instance, you might want to gather a day's worth of data every couple of weeks and whenever you add devices or reconfigure the network. Comparing these different snapshots of network traffic can alert you to potential problems *before* they turn into bottlenecks. As with network errors, if you do find potential traffic problems, you may need to reconfigure the network. For example, you might find it necessary to install a router to isolate traffic flow in a particular area.

Some of this information can be collected in real time. You can also save the data you collect and create summary graphs and charts for quick analysis of traffic patterns. For example, you can generate charts that show which users access shared devices and how frequently they access them. Or you can generate a chart to identify peak periods of network activity.

If you have an internet, you should also routinely examine traffic crossing the routers. This type of analysis is important for peak internet performance. If you find excessive traffic crossing a router, this might suggest a problem with the distribution of services or users among connected networks. You can try to correct this problem by relocating or adding servers, printers, or computers, or by restructuring the affected networks to balance traffic more evenly among various routers in the internet.

As shown in the following figure, AppleTalk Internet Router software shows you the number of packets received and forwarded by the router, and is an indicator of the router's overall usage. The Internet Router's Recent Activity Rate meter shows you the current level of traffic moving through the router.

Network Information for Router: AppleTalk Internet Router					
Packets Routed:	24		Network Reliability:	100.0%	
Recent Activity Rate:	Idle Busy		Recent Network Error Rate:	Low High	

10 zones, 9 networks sorted by: **Zone Name**

	Network Range		Zone Name	Distance		Forwarding Port	Next Router
		40	Accounting	0		LocalTalk	(91)
		61	LocalTalk Zone	1		LocalTalk	195
		62	LocalTalk Zone	2		LocalTalk	195
		63	LocalTalk Zone	0		LocalTalk	(166)
	25 –	35	Marketing...	0		EtherTalk	(27, 33)
	45 –	55	Publications	0		TokenTalk	(47,207)
	2200 –	2203	TTLabZone1	2		LocalTalk	195
	2300 –	2303	TTLabZone3	2		LocalTalk	195
	58 –	60	Zone1...	2		LocalTalk	195

Remote administration

Using a utility such as Timbuktu (from Farallon Computing), you can perform some administrative tasks remotely from your own computer. Such a utility lets you view and operate another computer on the network, such as a file server or a user's computer.

Remote administration can be useful in a number of ways. For one, it's simply easier not having to walk over to a server for routine administrative tasks, such as registering users. This is especially convenient if your server is located in a locked room or is located far away from your office. Yet another advantage from a network service standpoint is that you can remove the monitor, keyboard, and video card from a file server (for security or economic reasons) and still be able to administer the server from your own computer.

Helping a user with Timbuktu

In addition, remote administration is useful for helping users who may not be located near you. (Training and support is an important part of your role, and is discussed later in this chapter.) If users are having problems, you can take a look at exactly what's on their screens—and perhaps even fix the problem—without leaving your chair. You can also give a group of users an on-screen demonstration, and everyone can remain at their own computers. Some remote-administration software even enables you to view and control other computers over phone lines, making long-distance remote administration possible as well.

To perform remote administration, you install special software on your computer and on the computers you want to administer remotely. The software provides users with ultimate control over who can view or control their computers—users must give you access privileges before any remote administration can take place.

◆ **Note** If you use remote software to administer a file server, be aware that some products send your administrator password in **clear text**—in unencrypted form—as it's transmitted on the network. This means that someone with a monitoring program or device could potentially intercept the password. ◆

Generating network reports

Network reports provide you with valuable information about how the network is being used. You can use these reports to analyze the current state of network activity and then file them in your network logbook for later reference and comparison. You can generate network reports by using administrative tools, such as Inter•Poll, or through network service software, such as print service, file service, and E-mail service.

In the previous section, you learned about the device list and system information list that can be generated using Inter•Poll. When printed, these two reports become useful historical references. Inter•Poll allows you to customize these reports so that they are more meaningful to you. For instance, if your network has no zones, you might want to change the device list format to eliminate the zone column.

Most network services also produce reports. The AppleShare File Server provides detailed information to help you monitor how the server is being used and to help you make decisions about the amount of shared disk space needed. A Server Report lists all connected volumes and shows the space available on each. It also lists registered users, shows what groups they belong to, and tells you how many folders and files each user maintains and how much disk space the files occupy. A Volume Report lists the folders on a volume, the names of their enclosed files and folders, and the access privileges, owner, and associated group for each folder.

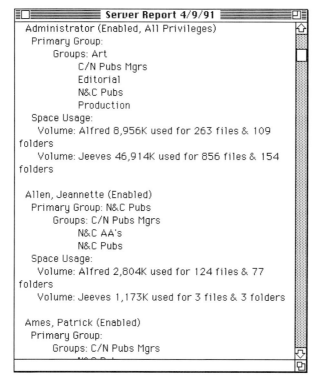

An AppleShare File Server report

The AppleShare Print Server provides a report that details information about all documents printed through the server. The report shows the name of the document, who printed it, when it was printed, how many pages it was, if it was completed, and whether a printing error occurred.

Print Spooler Log						
Status	Document	User	Date/Time		Pages	
Completed	Read Note	Gary Henry	4/24/91	1:30:59 PM	1	
			4/24/91	1:31:40 PM	1	
Completed	buddy info	Regello, Carol...	4/24/91	1:41:49 PM	2	
			4/24/91	1:43:11 PM	2	
Completed	Monthly Report	Marcus Jordan	4/24/91	2:09:09 PM	6	
			4/24/91	2:11:22 PM	6	
Completed	09 Ch. 5/Selecting	Sondra Garcia	4/24/91	2:09:54 PM	10	
			4/24/91	2:15:45 PM	10	
Completed	• Ledger Entry •	Patterson, Ja...	4/24/91	2:20:41 PM	1	
			4/24/91	2:21:02 PM	1	
Completed	net style sheet	Diane Goulder	4/24/91	2:22:37 PM	2	
			4/24/91	2:23:26 PM	2	
Completed	Read Me Before Installing!	Gary Henry	4/24/91	2:34:54 PM	9	
			4/24/91	2:37:11 PM	9	
Completed	7.0InternalRolloutUpdate...	Gary Henry	4/24/91	2:36:41 PM	7	
			4/24/91	2:38:23 PM	7	
Completed	• Ledger Entry •	Patterson, Ja...	4/24/91	2:38:37 PM	1	
			4/24/91	2:39:01 PM	1	
Completed	Troubleshooting caveats	Gary Henry	4/24/91	2:40:19 PM	12	
			4/24/91	2:43:29 PM	12	

An AppleShare Print Server report

The print server report is a good way for you to monitor printer activity and performance. It can also be used for such practical purposes as tracking missing documents. For instance, if a document was picked up by another user by mistake, the report shows who used the printer before and after the missing document was printed. In addition, the report can be used for internal billing purposes, since it shows who used the printer, when they used it, and how long they used it.

An E-mail report typically lists the date, time, sender, receiver, and subject for all messages transmitted through the network mail system. As with the print server report, the E-mail report can help you monitor the amount of mail activity on the network and tell you the source of the activity.

Backing up and restoring shared files

Any number of situations can lead to lost data—from human error to hard disk malfunctions. If an organization loses information, it can be a disaster. Even if the information is reproducible, spending time to research and re-create lost data can seriously affect a company's work flow. Backing up shared files stored on network servers is one of the most important functions you'll perform as the network administrator. You can reduce your organization's risk by following a routine backup schedule that suits your network's specific needs. For critical information, it's important to keep backup copies off-site in case the original backups are destroyed.

To back up files on the file server, you'll probably use a backup utility program. Although you can use the Finder to back up files (by simply clicking and dragging), the Finder is not designed to back up large amounts of information, so backing up files using just the Finder can be a slow process. In addition, the Finder does not preserve **file server attributes,** such as folder ownership and access privileges of folders on a file server. Some backup utilities are specifically designed for copying server volumes or folders, and can be very fast. In addition, many utilities preserve server attributes and provide other conveniences such as timed, automatic backups.

Types of backups

There are two kinds of backup methods: volume and file-by-file. A **volume backup** (also referred to as a *mirror* or *image backup*) creates an exact duplicate of all data on the file server volumes. A volume backup is fast for backing up an entire hard disk. Using this method, you must back up the entire volume at one time. You cannot selectively back up individual files or only those files that have changed since the last backup. Similarly, when restoring data, you must restore the entire volume to a hard disk with the same or greater capacity.

A **file-by-file backup** creates copies of individual files, one at a time. One type of file-by-file backup, called an **incremental backup,** saves data that has been created or modified since the last backup was done. Because much of the information on the server does not usually change often (such as applications, old files, the system folder, and desk accessories), this selective backup feature can save you a lot of time and backup space. File-by-file backup also allows you to restore files individually onto a disk of any capacity. If you purchase a file-by-file backup utility, be sure to get one that preserves file server access attributes; some do not provide this capability.

The most effective backup schemes combine volume and file-by-file backups. For instance, you may want to do a weekly volume backup to back up an entire volume and make an incremental backup every day to back up shared files that change daily. The pros and cons of volume and file-by-file backups are summarized in the list below.

Volume backup advantages

Easy to perform.

Faster for backing up an entire hard disk.

Restores an entire hard disk in case of failure.

Less prone to user errors, since individual files are not selected.

Excellent for archive copies.

Copies server attributes.

Volume backup disadvantages

Does not recognize data by folder or file.

Must be restored to a hard disk with the same or greater capacity.

Restores the original fragmentation of all files.

Can't restore a single file.

File-by-file backup advantages

Very useful for restoring single files.

Copies individual files quickly.

Can selectively copy modified files.

Restores onto a hard disk of any capacity.

Assists in correcting disk fragmentation.

File-by-file backup disadvantages

Some utility programs may not copy server attributes.

Slow for copying an entire hard disk.

Backup media

You can make backup copies on tape, floppy disks, hard disks, or optical disks. Many backup utilities come with their own backup device (such as a tape unit), and may require that you use only that device for backup. Other utilities allow some flexibility in the type of media that can be used. When evaluating the best backup media for your network, you need to consider such factors as cost, speed, convenience, and operating ease. Regardless of the backup media you use, be sure to maintain a strict labeling and filing system to keep track of the data on the media. Mark each tape or disk clearly and record the backup information in your logbook. If you store the backup copies on-site, it's wise to keep them safeguarded in a fireproof safe.

Tape is a commonly used backup medium. Tape drives are usually cost-effective, especially if you have several file servers or volumes to back up. As disk storage on the network increases, backups take longer and usually require multiple cartridges or cassettes. Tape units are now available with single cassette capacity of hundreds or thousands of megabytes, which can make tape backup easier and faster. Be aware, however, that with increased capacity comes increased cost. You can use the same tape drive unit for the entire network, but use different tape cassettes for each volume. A good tape drive unit has software that includes both volume and file-by-file backup and restoration.

Floppy disks are the least expensive backup solution because you don't have to buy an additional hard drive or tape unit. However, if you have to back up large amounts of information, floppy disks are impractical; the amount of information each disk can hold is limited, and you'll have to swap disks frequently while the copying is in progress.

Hard disks are a faster alternative to floppy disks, but they can be expensive. In addition, hard disks are vulnerable to failure, so they may not be as secure as tape. If you choose to use a hard disk as the backup medium, it must have at least as much storage capacity as the volume you're backing up.

Optical disks are a relatively new alternative for backup media. They can store hundreds of megabytes and are easy to remove and transport. However, backup can be slow and the optical disks can be expensive.

Once you decide which kind of backup media you need, you'll need to consider how it will be used. To keep media costs down, you'll probably want to use some kind of **rollover method,** in which you use backup media for a scheduled period of time and then routinely reuse it for a new set of backups. A rollover schedule reduces the total number of disks or tapes required for routine backup. For instance, you may use a different backup tape each week for a fiscal quarter. Then, at the beginning of the next quarter, you'll reuse the tapes from the previous quarter, starting with the first tape.

For easier backup management, you'll also need to consider how to segment backups. For example, you may want to back up each server volume onto a separate tape rather than back up all of the volumes onto a single large tape. This makes it much easier to locate and retrieve information when you need it. If you have a single volume, consider backing up users' folders alphabetically by last name; for example, putting users A–I on one tape, users J–R on a second tape, and users S–Z on a third tape.

You may also need to make **archive backups,** which are volume or file-by-file backups stored for historical purposes. Archive copies are usually required to maintain records of business activity for a period of four or more years; the copies are normally secured off-site or in a vault.

Be aware that both tapes and disks wear with repeated use. Consider discarding these media occasionally, erasing the data (with a magnetic eraser) for security reasons prior to disposal.

Backup schedules

By consulting with network users, you can create a practical backup schedule based on these considerations:

- *Importance and volatility of the data.* Consider how difficult, time-consuming, and expensive it would be to re-create the data if it is lost. Give special consideration to volatile data—data that is frequently changed. The more important and volatile the data, the more frequently you should do backups. Data that is considered critical and volatile should be backed up daily.

- *Backup responsibilities assumed by the users.* Most users consider their shared data to be important and volatile, but time constraints may make it impractical for you to perform backups as often as users would like you to. Encourage users to back up their own shared files to floppy disks or to tape (using a departmental tape unit) on a regular basis. Having those additional server backup copies prevents the loss of data that could occur between your regularly scheduled backups.

- *Length of time the data must be retained.* In every business, different information must be saved for varying periods of time. Some employment information must be retained for years, while other information may get saved for only a fiscal quarter. Determining the retention requirements for the information stored on your file servers will help establish the backup schedule you need.

- *Size and number of file server volumes.* Even when the volatility of material indicates the need to back up frequently, the sheer quantity of data on the hard disk may make it impractical for you to do this (and budgeting constraints may make make it impractical for you to buy several backup units). For example, in a situation where volatile data is kept on six 80-megabyte volumes, a great deal of time would be spent making a daily volume backup. This is a situation where users may have to help out by making incremental backups of their own files on the server.

Because work environments are dynamic, it's a good idea to assess these factors periodically to see if any have changed, requiring you to alter your backup schedule.

You may want to consider the following backup schedules, or a combination of these, when developing a schedule for your own network:

- *Daily.* A daily backup schedule includes incremental backups of new or changed data only. Daily schedules are normally used for important or frequently changed data. While they are the best insurance against lost data, they can be time-consuming if you have to perform the backups yourself. Asking users to assume some responsibility for backing up their own shared files may be a viable alternative.

- *Weekly.* A weekly backup schedule is either a volume backup or an incremental backup of data created or changed since the last volume backup. This backup schedule is often used by network administrators for general purpose data security.

- *Quarterly.* A quarterly backup schedule is a volume backup performed every fiscal quarter. This backup schedule is commonly used to capture data that will be archived for historical reference.

Let's look at a few examples of backup schemes. These examples are meant as guidelines—there are no absolutes when creating a backup schedule. The schedule you create, though based on similar information, might differ.

Example 1

A large talent management business creates a monthly database related to all clients it represents, based on input from all talent managers. This information is shared by all department members, so it goes on the file server on a 160-megabyte hard disk. The data is crucial to the company's success and changes are made daily. Individual managers make copies of the records for their own clients, but they don't back up the shared databases on the server. The original must be retained as long as the business is in operation, and archive copies are kept in a secure vault.

Backup considerations

Importance and volatility	High
User responsibilities	Some
Data retention	Long
File server disk size	Large

Backup strategy: The administrator of this talent management network has decided that a weekly volume backup with a midweek incremental should capture all of the information. Although a daily incremental would provide more security, it may not be practical due to the size of the hard disk. Since users take responsibility for backing up the files for their own clients, data is secure.

Example 2

The Personnel department of XYZ company has standard forms for travel, benefits, new equipment requests, and so forth. The original forms are kept on the file server, and must be retained "forever." They can easily be re-created and seldom change. The forms occupy a small space on the file server's 40-megabyte hard disk. A signed hard copy of each completed form is kept by Personnel.

Backup considerations

Importance and volatility	Low
User responsibilities	No
Data retention	Long
File server disk size	Small

Backup strategy: The network administrator has decided that this data will be captured in each week's regular volume backup. Additional backup is not required, since this information can easily be recovered from the copy stored in Personnel.

Example 3

Middle managers at a financial holding company produce a weekly shared report that is retained for three months. The information is critical and changes frequently. Managers are responsible for backing up their input to the file server. Final copies are on the file server on a moderate-size hard disk.

Backup considerations

Importance and volatility	High
User responsibilities	Yes
Data retention	Moderate
File server disk size	Medium

Backup strategy: The administrator of this network has decided on a combination backup schedule: a weekly incremental backup, reusing the incremental tape every month, and a monthly volume backup, reusing the volume tape every three months.

Backing up the server locally and over the network

There are two ways you can back up a server: locally and over the network. Backing up locally means shutting down the server and backing up files to a device (such as a hard disk or tape unit) attached directly to the server. Backing up over the network means that you can back up the server while it is running. You log on to the file server from a computer and back up the server remotely to a unit attached to the computer. (Note that a faster network, such as Ethernet, will provide faster network backup.) The backup program you use determines which kind of backup you can perform.

If you use a backup program that requires you to shut down the server, you can minimize the interruption by scheduling backups before or after regular work hours or on weekends. In general, try to schedule backups at the same time each day or week, notifying users when the backup will occur. Most programs that back up the file server locally do copy AppleShare attributes (such as folder ownership). However, some programs that back up the server over the network do not copy these attributes, requiring you to reassign them if you need to restore the files.

◆ **Note** If you want to back up the server over the network and you're concerned about data security, make sure that the product you use encrypts files as they're transmitted. Some products that back up data over the network transmit files in clear text—in unencrypted form—which means that the files could be intercepted with a monitoring program or device. ◆

When you back up the server locally, users can't access the server.

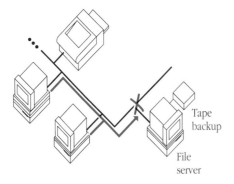

When you back up the server over the network, access to the server is uninterrupted.

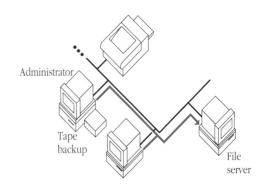

Backing up user files
on individual computers

It's important not only to back up shared files on the server, but also to encourage users to back up the information on their own computers. You might want to set up a standard procedure to make it easy for them to do backups. For example, establish a routine so that every week the departmental tape backup unit is passed around from person to person.

Alternatively, you can use a backup utility, such as Retrospect Remote (from Dantz Development Corporation), that enables users to automatically back up their local disks over the network to the file server. (This can be the same utility you use to back up file server volumes over the network.) You may want to set up a separate volume on your server for just this purpose. Some products enable users to specify the exact time of backup, which is convenient if users would rather perform the backup when they're away from their desks or during nonbusiness hours. In addition, some products enable you to automatically initiate backups of each user's computer onto a backup unit attached to the file server—a handy feature if you need to ensure regular backup of user data.

Supporting and training users

Experienced administrators will probably tell you that the majority of "network problems" are *not* caused by faulty hardware or software but by *user error.* This is good news for you, since you can readily control this aspect of network operation by setting up a routine training program for all users. Let users know (especially the reluctant "I can do it myself" types) that it's your job to make sure everyone is using the network in the same way with the same information.

Training users will give them a sense of comfort and will make your job a lot easier in the long run. Users need to understand what the network is for, what the various components are, and what they should and should not do. Training not only helps avert user errors; it also helps you solve problems more quickly when troubleshooting, since everyone will be speaking the same networking language. For example, an informed user might specifically say to you, "The mail server is missing from the Chooser," rather than a naive statement such as "The network is down."

Conduct training in whatever way works best for you: one-on-one sessions, small classes, demonstrations, and so on. Keep a library of manuals in your office for the products used on your network. Users may want to borrow these or you may choose to excerpt specific material from the manuals to distribute to users in the form of summaries, check lists, quick reference cards, and updates. Keep in touch with your users to let them know about changes to the network, such as new zones, additional or renamed printers or servers, or new site-licensed software on the file server.

Provide users with specific training in the following areas:

- *Background concepts and terminology.* Help users understand "what's in it for them." Explain what a network is, what the various servers do, and how the network will help them with specific tasks. When they learn how much the network can streamline their everyday work, cooperation will be a natural result.

- *Procedures.* Explain such procedures as logging on and off a file server, opening folders and files, saving and backing up files, reporting network problems, and user courtesies (such as printing large documents at less busy times of the day).

- *Users' responsibilities.* Teach users to check with you first before adding any equipment or software to the network. Adding unauthorized hardware or software can affect network operation and security and can also have legal ramifications (in the case of software licensing infringements). Ask users to keep you informed of all network problems in order to keep operations running smoothly and let them know about established procedures for reporting problems. Users should also know what to do when you're not available. You will probably want to designate someone as an alternate administrator so that users have a secondary contact to help them.

- *Equipment.* Explain how each piece—the cable, connectors, computers, servers, and so on—operates as part of the network. Show users how equipment connects and disconnects from the network (a common source of network problems!) and advise them about such things as not stepping on cables beneath their desks.

- *Operations.* Explain such network operations as how to use file service, shared applications, E-mail, the departmental backup unit, and how to perform simple maintenance chores such as refilling the paper tray on the LaserWriter printer.

- *Security.* Ensure that each user understands the security concerns of the network. They should understand why password confidentiality is critical, how security might be breached, and how to protect the network from possible virus infection.

After the initial training, you may want to consider providing users with some kind of written troubleshooting guidelines, which they can review before calling you with problems. Some administrators have gotten quite creative with this idea, providing interactive HyperCard® stacks that tell users how to solve common problems.

User training scenarios

Here are a few examples to illustrate what might happen with and without user training.

Example 1

An important aspect of security training is informing all users that loading unauthorized software on the network can seriously affect security. The following users both find an interesting application on an electronic bulletin board and want to load it on the file server.

Untrained user: This user puts the application on the file server. Later that day, the administrator is plagued with complaints from users about a variety of network problems. The administrator has ruled out the usual sources of network problems, then finds out that this user has downloaded unauthorized software to the server. The server may be infected with a virus.

Trained user: This user knows that downloading software from a bulletin board service and putting it on the file server can be risky. She first downloads the application directly to a floppy disk and runs it on the virus-checking station to scan for potential virus infection. When she learns it's free from viruses, she then copies the application to the file server.

Example 2

Educating users about the various equipment on the network is essential. The following users are planning a software demonstration and need to find another Macintosh computer right away.

Untrained user: This user finds a Macintosh computer sitting on a table outside his office. He assumes it's an extra, and disconnects it from the network. After the demonstration, he brings the computer back to the table and then sits down at his own computer to do some work on the file server. After repeated attempts to find the file server in the Chooser, he calls the network administrator, complaining about the network being down. After a brief investigation, the administrator finds the problem— the file server is the disconnected Macintosh sitting on the table outside the user's office!

Trained user: This user knows, from the training he received, that the computer located outside his office is a file server. He asks the administrator if he can borrow a computer for the demonstration.

Example 3

Educating users about how the equipment is connected to the network can prevent common network mishaps. The following users are going on a business trip and decide to disconnect their Macintosh Portable computers from the network.

Untrained user: At the end of the day, Michael unplugs his computer from the network by simply disconnecting the connector box from the LocalTalk cable. The next day, the administrator receives complaints from users about not being able to access network services. After a brief investigation, the administrator discovers that the network has a break in it—the problem is the missing connector box in Michael's office.

Trained user: To remove her Macintosh computer from the network, Alyssa disconnects the cable from the back of the computer, leaving the connector box in place. As long as the connector box is left, Alyssa knows that the network connection remains intact.

Upgrading system software

Part of network maintenance is upgrading the system software as new versions become available. Updated system software typically provides new capabilities and should be installed on all network devices—computers and servers—at the same time. From an administrative standpoint, it's a good idea to make sure that all like devices are running the same versions of system software. For one thing, this consistency provides you with a more controlled environment—users are running the same system software with the same applications—minimizing the opportunity for problems to arise. In addition, different versions of some system software, such as LaserWriter driver versions, may cause a variety of network conflicts.

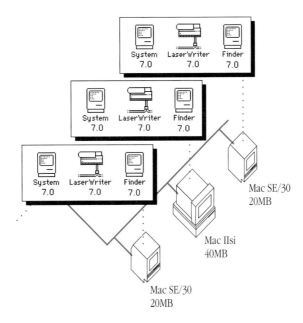

There are basically seven steps to a system upgrade:

1. Schedule the upgrade with users. It's important to let users know when you're going to upgrade system software. You might want to send them an E-mail message, telling them that you'll need to get on their computers for about ten minutes. Give them a date and approximate time. Also, let them know when servers will be down for the upgrade and for how long.

2. Make sure that users' data has been backed up. You can pass around the departmental backup unit or remind users to back up to the file server before the upgrade takes place.

3. Upgrade system software for network services.

4. Upgrade system software for each computer.

5. Verify the installation using a software tool such as Inter•Poll. Check separately for system version, Finder version, and LaserWriter driver version.

6. Record the system software update in your network logbook, carefully noting all software version numbers.

7. Train users. Explain any new features and capabilities of the new system software to each of the network users.

For more information about upgrading your network to Macintosh System 7, see the *System 7 Group Upgrade Guide* that comes with the System 7 Group Upgrade Kit from Apple Computer.

Adding users and network services

This section provides an overview of the process used to add users and network services to your network. This process will go very smoothly if you adopt a simple three-phase strategy: preparation, installation, and follow-up. This strategy can apply to new networks as well as to existing ones that are being modified.

Adding users

Preparation

The first step in adding a new user is identifying the user's needs for network services, such as printing and file sharing, as well as the user's software needs and primary workgroup. Also determine the user's needs for specific training and for shared file backup. Then, identify the location of the new user within the network. Using the network map, identify which office or cubicle the new user is going to occupy. Determine where the computer will be located within that office area.

Next, identify the cable requirements for the installation. Referring to the network map and examining the new office can help you determine these requirements. Installation may require laying new cable or it may involve simply plugging in the computer to existing cable.

Finally, try to determine the potential impact of adding the user to the network. Check to see that the addition does not exceed any node limit or cable length restrictions or involve a significant increase in demand for network services. If these problems arise, consider redesigning your network. For example, you may need to add or relocate shared resources or add a router to isolate network traffic.

Installation   Installation is the phase when you connect the user's hardware and install all necessary software. Before scheduling installation, consult with your network users; adding new equipment may force you to disconnect cables, resulting in a temporary loss of network services.

With the new computer turned off, connect the network cables to the appropriate LocalTalk, Ethernet, Token Ring, or other AppleTalk-compatible network connector. You can then install the appropriate system software and any necessary network drivers and interface cards. Next, test the computer using the Chooser to verify that the computer is active on the network. If you have installed the computer properly, it should now have access to all network printers.

The final installation steps involve adding the user to all network services, including file service, mail service, and print service. Install any network service software on the user's computer, if required. Then, register the new user's name on the appropriate network service list (running the network services application on your own computer). Give the new user the required passwords for these services. Finally, test the new user's access to network services. For instance, make sure the user can log on to file servers, send a message through E-mail, and print to the print server.

Follow-up   After the installation is complete, be sure to update your network map and logbooks. Then train the new user, explaining how to access network services, where printers are located, proper network "etiquette" (such as printing large documents during off-hours), and so forth. Make sure the new user has access to necessary documentation, such as software manuals. You may also want to notify other users so that they can add the new user to their E-mail lists and groups.

Adding network services

Preparation

When you're assessing the need for a network service, talk to users to identify common workgroup needs and individual needs and to get an overall picture of the type of network traffic you can expect on the network. Using your network map, identify the network and zones that need the new service.

Next, determine the potential impact of implementing the new service. If you're adding the service to an existing network, ensure that it is not going to make your network exceed its capacity in any area. You can determine whether or not this will happen by projecting the new service and its accompanying cable, power, and node requirements onto your network map.

Finally, identify the optimum placement of the devices necessary for the service within the selected zone. Remember, you'll want to place shared devices, such as servers and printers, in a location that is convenient, secure, and that maximizes network performance. Refer to the section "Where to Place Shared Resources" in Chapter 7 for more information.

Installation

Installation is the phase when you connect devices to the network and install the necessary software. If you're adding a service to an existing network, first consult with your network users, because you may need to disconnect some devices temporarily while you connect a new server or printer. Connect the new device to the network cable and set up any necessary server software on the device. Then test the new service from your own computer to be certain that you've set it up properly. Finally, install the appropriate client software on all computers that need to access the service.

Follow-up

After you install the new service, update your network map and logbook. Then train users on how to use the new service.

Managing your servers

The following sections cover some important aspects of managing network servers: organizing information on the file server; freeing up shared disk space; checking server security; and using applications on the server, which includes issues such as server compatibility and copyright and licensing considerations.

Organizing information on the file server

Information stored on a file server needs to be organized so that users can find what they need quickly. Because the server is a repository of information for a large number of people, it can rapidly become a hodgepodge of assorted folders and files. Although users can (and should) create their own individual folders, you might consider taking charge of at least the "top level" view of the server to lay a foundation of order for the folders and files nested within.

Organize the information as intuitively as you can, labeling folders with names that are meaningful to those who need to access them. Periodically check through server volumes to ensure that folders are appropriately named and logically grouped.

Consider organizing folders into these categories:

- *Public folders.* You can use these folders to store documents and applications that all users need to share. If users should not make changes to files within a public folder, you can specify that the folder is read-only. For instance, you can place contracts or forms in a read-only folder. Users can copy these forms to their own hard disks without altering the originals.

- *Group folders.* These folders allow you to restrict access to users you specify. You can set up departmental group folders that contain files and folders most commonly used by members of a particular department. You can also set up collaborative group folders for projects where users from several departments are working together and need to share information.

- *Individual drop folders.* These are private folders that can serve as mailboxes for each user. Files and folders placed in an individual's drop folder can be seen by the individual but not by anyone else. This is a very efficient way to exchange files.

You might consider locking this top level of the server (the "root") so that users must place folders within one of the top level folders you create. This preserves the order you've established, and prevents users from arbitrarily moving or copying files or folders to the top level, creating a disorganized assortment of information.

File Server

Public folders	Group folders	Drop folders
BULLETIN BOARD	Art Group	Sondra's Drop Box
Licensed Software	Writer's Group	Steve's Drop Box
Manager's Calendar	Production Group	John's Drop Box
Boilerplate Materials	Managers	Joyce's Drop Box
Print Specs		Debbie's Drop Box
Clip Art Files		Contractor's Drop Box

Since creating group folders and groups may be a common task for you, you might want to design a request form to make it easier for you to track requests from users. The form should note who is making the request, as well various information about the group and folder. A sample form is shown on the next page.

Network Administration Work Request Form

Requestor: _____ Extension _____ Date _____

Location: _____

■ *To set up a new AppleShare group*

New Group name: _____ Volume name: _____

Names in group: _____ _____

Approximate timeframe for group: _____

■ *To add a folder to top level of AppleShare file server*

New folder name: _____ Volume name: _____

Users/groups having access: _____ _____

■ *To assign privileges to folder*

Read/Write ☐   Read only ☐   None ☐

Purpose of folder: _____

Approx. disk space needed: _____ Backup requirements: _____

Freeing up disk space

Over time, your servers can become cluttered with information that is difficult to find or outdated—taking up valuable disk space on the server. Try to check server contents routinely to weed out documents and applications that are no longer needed. Some files can probably be deleted; others can be archived to free up disk space. Always check with the owner before you move or delete a document. You can use server reports to see if users are unnecessarily keeping multiple copies of documents on the server or if many users keep the same application in a private folder on the server. It may be more efficient to use a multi-launch application that several users can open at the same time. Keep E-mail messages on the server for a set period, and let users know what this period is; then archive the messages or delete them.

Checking security

If you allow guests to log on to your server, you should occasionally log on as a guest yourself and examine the volumes to see what files and folders are visible. It's not uncommon for users to make access privileges too lenient; for example, by giving *See Files* and *See Folders* privileges to *Everyone*.

Using applications on a file server

There are several issues to consider when using applications on a file server. First, is the application compatible with the server? Second, if the application is compatible, how many people can open or **launch** it at the same time? And can more than one person work on a file at the same time? Third, what are the copyright and licensing agreements for this piece of software? Can one copy of the software be stored on the server for many people to share or do you need to purchase one copy of the software for each user? These issues are discussed in the following sections.

File server compatibility

Applications can be divided into the following compatibility categories:

- *Runs locally with the server.* Most applications can run locally from a computer while the computer is connected to a file server. There are some rare applications, however, that will break the connection to the file server when the application is started from a local disk.

- *Can be launched from the server.* Many applications can be launched directly from the file server. This eliminates the need to copy the application to a user's computer. There is usually a limit to how many people can launch the application simultaneously (this limit is often one).

- *Allows documents to be opened from the server.* Most applications allow documents to be opened directly from the file server. Rare applications require users to copy documents to their local disks before opening them.

- *Provides document management.* Applications that provide document management keep track of open documents. Document management ensures that all changes to a document are saved when more than one user edits a document, and may also lock users out of a file that is currently being accessed by another user.

As Table 10-1 shows, when an application is compatible with the file server, it can run locally on a computer that is connected to the server and can also be launched from the server. Further, if the application is **file server–aware,** it provides document management to ensure the integrity of data.

If an application is compatible with the server, but is *not* file server–aware, then the application does not provide document management. There is often little or no control over who opens a file through that application. This means that if a user opens a document that is already in use, the user who saves changes to the document last will overwrite the changes made by the previous user, unintentionally destroying data. If an application is not file server–aware, you should place documents created from the application in private folders on the server or on a computer's local hard disk to eliminate the possibility of access by multiple users.

Table 10-1 File server compatibility categories

	Runs locally with server	**Launched from server**	**Open document from server**	**Provides document management**
Compatible and file server–aware	Yes	Yes	Yes	Yes
Compatible but not aware	Yes	Yes	Yes	No
Coexistence only	Yes	No	Yes	No
Incompatible	No	No	No	No

Launching applications from a server

Even though some applications can be launched from a file server, doing so can have its drawbacks. An application that takes several seconds to open on a local hard drive can take a minute or more to open on a heavily used network. In addition, running applications from a file server can cause excessive and often unnecessary traffic on a network because of constant communication between computers and the server.

Coexistence is another class of server compatibility. This means that the application can run locally with the server and documents created through the application can be opened from the server, but the application cannot be launched from the server and does not provide document management. Applications in this category should be stored on individual computers rather than on the file server. Documents created from these applications should be stored on users' computers or in private folders on the server.

Incompatible applications will not run on a computer while it is connected to a file server. Users should log off the file server before launching any incompatible applications. Fortunately, such applications are rare.

To determine if an application is compatible with your file server, check the documentation and data sheets that came with the software. (The documentation may refer to compatible applications in a number of ways, such as *network-aware, file server–aware,* or *AppleShare-aware.)* If you can't find the information this way, contact the software vendor or check with an authorized Apple dealer.

Determining launch and access characteristics

Compatible applications can be further defined to describe their launch and file access features, as shown in the following chart.

Single-launch, single-user applications

Only one person at a time can open the application on the server and only one person at a time can open a file or change it.

These applications should probably be run from a workstation's local hard disk since there are no significant advantages to running them from the file server.

Single-launch, multi-user applications

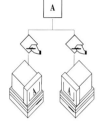

Only one person at a time can open the application, but two or more people can open or change the same file at the same time.

Many database applications fall into this category. Several people can work with the same file on the server while running their own copies of the application on their workstations. When one person makes a change to the file (such as updating a database record), the change can be seen by everyone accessing the file. Some multi-user applications let many users read a file at the same time, but allow only one person to modify the file at one time. These applications use a process called *file-locking* to prevent write-access by more than one person. Other multi-user applications actually allow several people to modify a file at the same time. These applications use record locking or byte-range locking, which locks specific portions of a file while it is being modified.

Multi-launch, single-user applications

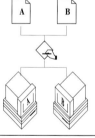

Two or more people can open a single copy of an application on the file server, but only one person at a time can open a particular file and change it.

Some word-processing programs operate in this manner. Place multi-launch applications in a public or group folder so that everyone can use it. Before placing the application on the file server, examine the license agreement to make sure that it is alright to do so.

Multi-launch, multi-user applications

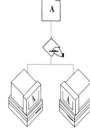

Two or more people can open a single copy of an application on the file server and two or more people can open or change the same file at the same time.

Some shared database programs, such as 4th Dimension (from ACIUS), fall into this category.

Copyright and licensing issues

Before placing an application on a file server (or in a shared folder of any kind), review the terms of the licensing agreement to ensure that it's alright to share the application. Licensing agreements vary widely, so take time to review each one.

An application may come with a single-copy license agreement or provide an option for site licensing. A **single-copy license** requires you to purchase one copy of the software for each computer on which you plan to use it. You will generally not be able to place such an application on the file server. A **site license** allows you to buy one copy of the software at a fixed rate for a certain number of computers (or sometimes on a per server basis for multi-user applications). If an application is site licensed, you can place one copy on the file server for many users to copy or share. Note, however, that having a site license does not usually mean *unlimited* use of the application within your organization.

Site licenses may not be cost effective for small organizations. However, in a larger organization, the fixed rate offered by the site license may be lower than purchasing a copy of the software for each individual. A site license also helps you "cover your bases" to ensure that everyone in your group has legal rights to use the software.

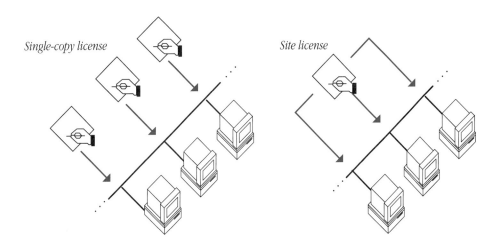

Single-copy license

Site license

Optimizing network performance

The day-to-day efficiency of a network depends on free-flowing traffic. Although you may have done your best at the planning stage to anticipate network traffic, you'll inevitably note performance problems as the network grows and increased demands are placed upon network services. You may receive complaints from users about network delays or notice problems yourself during routine monitoring of the network. It's the network administrator's role to identify and reduce bottlenecks to keep the network running at peak performance.

Excessive demand on services

Excessive traffic

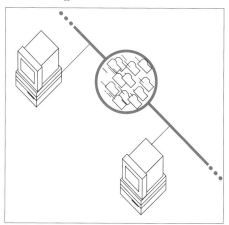

Bottlenecks fall into two general categories: those due to excessive traffic on the network and those due to excessive demand on network services. If the problem is excessive traffic, then the number of packets sent through the network media—the **throughput**—exceeds the media's capacity to handle it effectively. If a network service is overworked, the capacity of the media may be adequate, but the packets "back up" from the shared device much like cars at a stoplight. Eliminating bottlenecks may require you to take such steps as relocating equipment, adding new equipment (such as a router or server), or modifying network usage by simply changing user work habits.

Regardless of the type of bottleneck you may have on your network, there's a five-step analysis process you can use to identify and remove it.

Step 1

Identify the traffic sources on the network. Knowing the source of traffic puts you in a good position to reduce it. There's not much you can do to control overhead traffic sources, such as routers updating router tables. Instead, focus your attention on user-generated traffic sources; ask yourself *who* uses the network most often and *when* they use the network. To help identify these sources, you can use administrative traffic-monitoring software or router-monitoring software (for an internet).

Step 2

Examine network services to determine their load. On most networks, the majority of traffic flows between computers and shared devices such as file servers, printers, E-mail servers, and network modems. You can use network service reports and a variety of traffic summary charts (from a traffic-monitoring tool) to track changes in network service usage and to determine which users are accessing these services.

Step 3

Identify the traffic path. Use the network map to locate the identified sources and path of network traffic. The map can tell you if excessive traffic is coming from a certain department or work area. In more complex networks, the network map is essential for determining the traffic flow across routers and among various networks.

Step 4

Describe the activity between the traffic sources and network services. This step helps to establish who is doing what and when. In this step, you take information concerning specific traffic sources and network services and try to identify the type of activity that is generating the traffic. You can begin to describe network activity through the following tasks:

- *Talk with users.* This will help you uncover a wealth of information, such as the type of applications being used and when a given application or task (such as printing reports or billing) is performed. These discussions help you understand the organization's workflow and may identify certain periods of heavy traffic. Month-end billing, weekly payroll processing, or the afternoon generation of legal briefs are all examples of work that can generate periodic, heavy network traffic.

- *Re-examine data.* Look at traffic-monitoring data and network service reports again to see if usage patterns emerge. Does the activity follow any patterns? Does the use occur during certain times of day? Are some devices, such as a particular printer, being used significantly more than others?

Step 5

Recommend a solution. Your recommendation will be based on your analysis of the bottleneck and the activity causing it. Some possible solutions include the following:

- *Relocating existing network services.* In some situations, a network service or device receives little use and can be put to better use by relocating it elsewhere on the network or by connecting it directly to a user's computer, removing the device from the network. If a particular network service receives substantial traffic across a bridge or router, consider moving the service across the router. This keeps traffic isolated within a single network segment.

- *Adding network resources.* When complaints center on a specific network service, such as printing, adding new equipment may be the answer. As long as the overall capacity of the network is not exceeded, adding another shared device improves performance by splitting the workload.

- *Removing a network service from a server.* If you have too many network services running on the same server, users may experience a slowdown in services. For example, if you run the AppleShare File Server and Print Server on the same computer as the AppleTalk Internet Router, users may notice slowdowns in file and print service. If this is the source of the bottleneck, one solution would be to move the routing software to its own computer.

- *Changing users' network work habits.* This one may surprise you, but is sometimes the only solution needed. Users may not always use network services in the most efficient manner, generating unnecessary traffic congestion. For example, they may run software directly from the file server that could be run more easily and quickly from their own computers. Or they may print long reports during peak hours that could be printed at less busy times of the day.

- *Adding a router or changing to a faster network type.* In some situations, there may be a clear performance problem, but you are unable to identify any single traffic source, network service, or activity as the cause. In these situations, your network capacity may be stretched to the limit and the network may require some redesign. Adding a router and dividing the network into two subnetworks—each with its own network resources—may eliminate the problem. Or, you may need to switch to a faster network type, such as Ethernet, to accommodate your growing network needs.

Examples of performance analysis

The administrators in the following examples use the five-step analysis process to find solutions to each of their network problems.

Example 1

After installing a router, the traffic flow at J.L. Hanson, Inc., improved substantially. The firm has been divided into two zones, Admin and Marketing. Recently, however, the administrator has been receiving complaints from users in the Admin zone about slow performance. The administrator analyzes the situation:

Identify traffic sources. Using the router software, the administrator notices a large amount of traffic crossing the router from the Marketing zone into the Admin zone. She needs to find out why this is happening.

Examine network services. Using traffic summary charts, the administrator looks at network service usage. She notices that the network modem shows heavy traffic coming from the router. She also sees that the router shows heavy use by three people: Charlotte, Russ, and Manuel. They may be responsible for the increase in modem traffic.

Identify traffic path. The network map shows that these three users are in the Marketing zone and must cross the router to get to the network modem in the Admin zone.

Describe the activity. The administrator talks to her users. She finds that users in the Admin zone have little need for the shared modem. Those in the Marketing zone—especially Charlotte, Russ, and Manuel—have a frequent need for the modem.

Recommend a solution. The most cost-effective solution is to move the modem to the Marketing zone. This keeps traffic within that zone and out of the Admin zone.

Example 2

The administrator receives numerous complaints from users about printing delays. He takes the following steps to investigate and alleviate the problem:

Identify traffic sources. The administrator uses a traffic-monitoring program to analyze traffic during the course of the day. From a traffic summary chart, he sees that traffic seems pretty well distributed, although Sean, Rachel, Scott, and Adrian are using the network more than others.

Examine network services. Again, the administrator uses traffic summary charts and looks at file server and print spooler usage. He compares this usage with the previous month's and notices that LaserWriter use has increased substantially in comparison to other network services.

Identify traffic path. The administrator looks at the network map and locates the four users who appear to be the traffic source. Most are clustered in the Legal department.

Describe the activity. The administrator talks to users in the Legal department and discovers that they are printing large daily reports for a special project. He then examines the print spooler report from the laser printer, which confirms his discussions with users: the printer is receiving very heavy use.

Recommend a solution. Obviously, the increased printer demand has caused a printing bottleneck, with subsequent slowdowns for everyone trying to print. Because rescheduling the work for only certain times of day is not feasible, the administrator recommends leasing a printer for the Legal area until this project is done.

Example 3

The network administrator begins receiving complaints from users about delays of all kinds, including printing, accessing the file server, and sending E-mail. He does the following:

Identify traffic sources.   The administrator runs his traffic-monitoring software and produces a summary chart showing who's using the network. When he compares this chart to last week's, he notices unusually high traffic this week from Diana in the Production department.

Examine network services.   His traffic summary charts show a lot of file server access and a dramatic increase in file server usage this week compared to the week before.

Identify traffic path.   The administrator locates Diana and the file server on the network map.

Describe the activity.   He talks with Diana and finds out that she placed a graphics application on the file server this Monday and has been running the application directly from the server.

Recommend a solution.   The administrator asks Diana to download the application to her own hard disk. This removes the traffic source from the network, eliminating the congestion and overall delays.

Example 4

With the addition of a large new account, the volume of work has doubled and so has the traffic on the network. The administrator examines the network to see if she can improve performance.

Identify traffic sources. The administrator generates a traffic summary graph to assess who's using the network the most. Then she compares this graph to the one she generated last week. Although there is a definite increase in the volume of overall traffic, she can't find one source responsible for the increase.

Examine network services. When the administrator compares this week's network service usage with last week's, she notices an increase. However, the increase seems to be evenly distributed across all services.

Identify traffic path. The path of network traffic is difficult to trace. Users scattered throughout the network are generating more traffic.

Describe the activity. The administrator sits down with a vice-president in the firm to learn how the business is doing and to see how business might affect the network, now and in the short term. The vice-president tells her that the firm has experienced phenomenal growth—there has been a 50% increase in business this year and she anticipates substantial growth of about 20% in the upcoming year.

Recommend a solution. The administrator cannot find a specific cause of this traffic congestion. Given the current business conditions and the business forecast, she decides that a network redesign is in order. She studies the workflow and shared resource requirements of the group to determine where devices should be placed. She then divides the network into two by adding a router, improving performance on each connected network.

As you can see from these examples, there are many different causes of performance degradation, and each has its own corresponding solution. Making the right recommendation for removing bottlenecks requires a systematic approach, a solid understanding of your network, and a little experience. Discovering a workable solution is a lot like solving a puzzle—and the result can be just as satisfying.

11 Network Troubleshooting

Every network experiences problems at one time or another, whether from overloaded services, excessive network traffic, faulty equipment, or user error. Troubleshooting is the process of solving such problems by following a series of systematic, well-defined steps.

This chapter explores the following topics to help guide you through the troubleshooting process:

- administrative tools that can help you troubleshoot
- some of the most common network problems you may run across
- a step-by-step approach for solving network problems
- real-life troubleshooting scenarios that illustrate the concepts discussed in this chapter

Administrative tools

The tools introduced in Chapter 10 that perform everyday monitoring and maintenance are also useful for isolating and solving network problems. Your most basic diagnostic tools are the network map, network logbooks, and the Chooser.

You'll refer to the network map frequently, since it details the network layout and helps you find the precise location of network problems. It's important to keep your map current—each physical change to the network should be reflected on the map.

When a problem arises, your logbooks can help you identify any significant network addition or change that took place at roughly the same time the problem began—which might mean that the two are linked. For example, if someone filling in for you updates system software on Monday night and on Tuesday, users complain to you about not being able to print, the system upgrade noted in the logbook might be the cause. The logbook also enables you to find out if the problem has occurred previously and, if so, what steps were taken to solve it.

The Chooser is a quick way to determine whether network connections are functioning properly. If a device, such as a printer, does not show up in the Chooser, a potential problem may exist on the path between the user's computer and that device.

Other helpful troubleshooting tools include products such as Inter•Poll, TrafficWatch, the AppleTalk Internet Router, and Timbuktu. As discussed in Chapter 10, these products perform a variety of diagnostic functions to help you isolate network problems. They can help identify missing devices, report on system software versions, test the integrity of network connections and transmissions, gauge the amount of traffic on the network, and help you perform remote administration. Many of these tools are often used in combination with one another. For example, you can use one tool to produce a device list and scan for missing devices and then consult the network map to identify the location of these missing devices.

In addition to these software tools, there are some simple hardware tools available to test cables and connectors electrically. Voltmeters and continuity checkers can help identify conditions such as breaks, shorts, improper voltage, or open circuits. Cable testers can tell you how long the network cable is. Electrical ground testers can check three-pronged electrical outlets and modular phone jacks for proper installation, and can help locate the loss of a ground wire—which can wreak electrical havoc on a network.

The kinds of tools mentioned above are the ones most commonly used on small- to medium-sized networks. Other tools more appropriate for managing and troubleshooting large internets include **protocol analyzers** and high-end cable testers called **time-domain reflectometers.** These are expensive and require advanced technical knowledge to use.

A protocol analyzer is specialized software or hardware that lets an administrator examine individual packets to uncover network problems. Protocol analyzers range in price from a few thousand dollars to $25,000 and are usually tailored to work on a particular network type (such as Ethernet or Token Ring). Although many of these tools have been made easier to use in recent years, they still require a solid understanding of network protocols to interpret the results.

A time-domain reflectometer (TDR) is a sophisticated piece of equipment that takes cable scanning one step farther than simple cable testers. In addition to identifying electrical problems, such as shorts or breaks, the TDR can quickly find the exact location of the problem. A TDR can also locate cable in walls, show if a cable has been crimped during installation, and measure cable segments to ensure that the installation is within cable guidelines.

Common network problems

While there are many problems that can occur on any network or internet, there are three types of problems that are most common:

- missing devices
- the intermittent appearance and disappearance of network services and devices
- performance degradation

The following sections take a look at the symptoms and possible causes for each of these network problems.

Missing device

A missing device is a node (server, printer, modem, or another computer) that cannot be "seen" from other nodes. The following are common symptoms of a missing device:

- Users report that they can't access a file server or print device (the missing device may be the file server or print server).

- Users report that they can't access another zone or network (the missing device may be the router connecting two networks).

- Users report that they can't send mail to other users (the missing device may be the mail server).

- Users report that they can't see anything on the network (the missing device may be the user's own computer).

- A device listing (from Inter•Poll, for example) does not match the network map or a previous device list.

The most obvious cause of a missing device is that the device is not turned on or is not functioning properly. For example, if users can't access another network, check that the bridge or router connecting the networks is turned on. The other common cause of a missing device is a break in the network connection. When a break occurs on the network, devices on opposite sides of the break can no longer communicate with anything on the network beyond the point of the break.

There are four principle kinds of network breaks, as shown in the following chart.

Network breaks

A break at the connector

If there is a break at the connector, the affected device becomes the network termination point for the side of the network that remains connected. Devices on this side may continue to operate properly, but they will have no contact with devices beyond the termination point. (See the next section, "Intermittent Loss of Services or Devices," for more information on cable termination.)

A severed cable

Although network cable is sturdy, it can be severed by extreme stress, such as moving heavy furniture over the cable.

Broken or damaged connector pins

Broken or damaged connector pins are commonly overlooked when searching for network breaks. When verifying the physical health of a device, always disconnect the connectors and check the condition of the pins.

Disconnected cable extenders

Cable extension connnectors, such as those used on LocalTalk networks, can become unplugged when they are moved, causing a network break to occur.

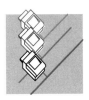

Intermittent loss of services or devices

The intermittent appearance and disappearance of network services or devices is called **ghosting.** Users may complain that a network device is available from the Chooser some of the time, but not always. Or, occasionally a device disappears from a device listing only to reappear moments later. Another symptom of ghosting is a noticeable increase in the number of cyclic redundancy check (CRC) errors uncovered during traffic monitoring.

Ghosting can be caused by any of the following conditions:

- *Too many devices.* You can connect up to 32 devices to a single LocalTalk network using the LocalTalk cable system. Ethernet networks specify a certain maximum number of devices per network segment and per network. Token Ring networks specify a certain maximum number of devices per ring. (Refer to Chapter 6 for details.) If you're having network problems, check the device limitations for your network type and the number of devices on your network to make sure that you're not exceeding the recommended limit. If necessary, subdivide the network using bridges or routers.

- *Improper network termination.* All bus networks must include terminating resistors to provide end points for the bus. If the network is not terminated properly, transmission problems will occur. The terminators for LocalTalk networks using the LocalTalk cable system are built into the connector boxes. A properly terminated LocalTalk network has no dangling cable extending beyond the last connector box, as shown below.

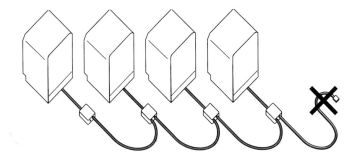

LocalTalk networks using the PhoneNET cable system are *not* self-terminating; you must add terminators on each end of the network cable.

There are different termination requirements for each kind of Ethernet medium. Traditional thin coaxial cable installations require separate terminators to make the network operational. The Apple Ethernet Thin Coax Transceiver and Apple Ethernet cable are self-terminating. If you have questions about the termination requirements of your network, refer to the appropriate installation instructions for your cable type.

■ *Loose connector contact.* When a network connection becomes loose without breaking completely, communication becomes intermittent between devices on both sides of the loose connection. Although most connectors lock into place, connections can loosen when devices are moved. (Note that the old AppleTalk Personal Network connectors do not lock and require retention devices to help secure cable connections.)

■ *Loose cable extenders.* Cable extenders can also become loose—especially nonlocking types—although no break in contact may be visible. When checking for intermittent connections, completely unplug and reconnect the cables to make sure there is firm contact.

■ *Damaged or obstructed cable.* A cable that has been damaged, pinched, or kinked may still be capable of intermittent throughput, with occasional breaks in transmission. This may be the most difficult network fault to detect if no external cable damage is visible. A network tool, such as Inter•Poll, may help isolate the area of damage or obstruction through loopback tests. In addition, cable testing devices, such as voltmeters and continuity checkers, may be useful in isolating the problem. If the cable in a particular location is damaged, you may need to replace it.

■ *Exceeded cable length limitations.* LocalTalk, Ethernet, and Token Ring networks each have limitations on the maximum cable lengths for each network segment. Going beyond these limitations can cause intermittent problems such as ghosting. Review the cable length specifications for your network and compare these to your network layout, using cable testing equipment if necessary. If your network exceeds the recommended cable lengths, install repeaters or subdivide networks by using bridges or routers.

- *Electromagnetic interference.* Running certain kinds of cable near sources of high electromagnetic interference, such as industrial machinery or power transformers, can cause intermittent transmission problems on the network. If you're using twisted-pair or coaxial cable and it's impractical to relocate equipment or reroute the cable, you may need to replace your existing cable with fiber-optic cable or use infrared light, both being very resistant to this type of interference.

- *Too many routers.* AppleTalk packets can traverse a maximum of 15 hops, at which point the packets are discarded. As this limitation is neared, ghosting symptoms may appear. If this is the source of ghosting, you may need to redesign your network to reduce the number of hops on your internet. Consider using a backbone for more efficient network routing.

Performance degradation

Performance degradation is an abnormal delay in network operations. The primary symptom is that users complain about a slowdown in network services, such as printing or file service. The following conditions can cause performance to degrade:

- *Excessive traffic.* You can use a traffic-monitoring tool and also talk to users about their network activities to gauge the traffic flow on the network. If traffic congestion is temporary, perhaps because of an abnormally busy week, you may need to ask users to access devices that aren't busy or access network services at different times of the day. If traffic congestion is a long-term problem, you may need to redesign the network by adding bridges or routers, adding a backbone network, or switching to a faster network type such as Ethernet.

- *Too few shared resources.* As your network grows, you may need to add shared resources, such as printers and servers. If you've been using shared printing on your network and users are experiencing slowdowns in printing, it may be time to add a print server to your network so that users can get on with other work after sending their documents to the printer.

- *Too many devices.* If you connect more than the recommended number of devices to your network, network segment, or ring, you may experience performance slowdowns. Again, you may need to subdivide your network by adding bridges or routers. (See Chapter 6 for details on recommended numbers of devices for each network type.)

- *System software conflicts.* Any device may cause network problems if it is operating with system software that differs from the standard version used on the network. Symptoms might be limited to the affected device or might affect network performance in other ways.

  You can verify software version numbers by using the About . . . command from the Apple (🍎) menu when working from an application or the Get Info command from the File menu when working from the Finder. You can also use an administrative tool, such as Inter•Poll, to check system software versions.

- *Driver incompatibility.* Most network service devices, including LaserWriter printers, file servers, and electronic mail servers, require that associated driver programs be installed on every computer using the service. All computers using a particular network service should have the same version of the driver installed. When a network service is slow to respond, the cause may be an incompatible software driver on the computer requesting the service. Usually, an error message will appear at the requesting computer indicating an incompatible driver version.

  Incompatible versions of printer drivers are a common occurrence. A user typically complains about receiving a message that the LaserWriter is reinitializing each time he or she prints a document. When this occurs, simply remove the driver on the user's computer, install the correct version that is consistent with the other network users, and then restart the computer. Again, tools such as Inter•Poll can be used to make sure that all computers are running the same versions of these driver files.

- *User error.* Don't overlook the possibility of user errors when looking for the source of performance problems. A reported slowdown in network performance may be caused by an inappropriate use of network services. For example, running a word-processing application from a file server instead of from a local hard disk may cause unnecessary slowdowns in individual—and network—performance.

- *Too many services on the same server.* If you're running several network services on the same server computer, users may experience a slowdown in network services. You may need to move a service, such as E-mail, to its own server, rather than running E-mail with file service and print service.

- *Too many routers.* If packets must travel near AppleTalk's maximum of 15 hops to get to their destination, performance degradation may occur. If you suspect that this is happening, redesign your network (perhaps with a backbone) to reduce the number of hops on the internet.

- *Viruses.* If the causes listed above fail to uncover the source of a performance degradation, check for possible virus infection on the computer of the user reporting the slowdown and on any affected servers. Remember always to check new software with a virus-detection program before loading it on the network (see Chapter 9 for a discussion of viruses).

Troubleshooting strategies

In an effort to solve a problem quickly, it may be tempting to make certain assumptions and simply jump right into the situation. This is seldom worthwhile, since it often leads to wasted time—or fails to solve the problem entirely. A more effective approach—and one that all successful troubleshooters use—is to follow a well-developed and properly implemented troubleshooting strategy that covers three steps:

1. Clearly define the symptoms of the problem by collecting the facts and verify that the problem is network related.
2. Isolate the problem using a top-down approach.
3. Check and correct any hardware or software problems at the localized device.

Step 1

Define the symptoms of the problem and verify that the problem is network related.

While all three troubleshooting steps are important, this step is vital to the rest of the process. Without a clear, concise definition of the problem, finding the solution is a haphazard, hit-or-miss approach. If more than one problem is being reported, define each one separately and work on one problem at a time. Sometimes multiple problems are related and the solution to one of them fits the others.

To define the problem, talk to users and document what is currently known about the problem. Keep in mind that symptoms are often poorly defined by users and that the problem and symptom frequently lie in totally different areas. To counter this, listen closely to what users say, paraphrasing and clarifying statements as they speak. Ask pointed questions that clearly define the problem in your mind. While going through this fact-finding process, make sure you address the possibility of *user error*. Many times a user is quick to judge a problem as software- or hardware-related, when, in reality, the user is at fault. For example, the user may have tried to access a network service without first selecting it in the Chooser. Talk to the user about the specific procedure followed and ask the user to reproduce the problem while you watch.

During this step, you'll verify that the problem is, in fact, network related. It's common for users to blame any unspecified problem on "the network." Before proceeding to network troubleshooting, be sure that the problem is really a network one.

A problem *is* network related when one or more of the following conditions exist:

- One or more devices cannot communicate.
- Network access or response is intermittent.
- A network service fails.
- The network experiences performance degradation. Devices run, but at a much slower-than-normal rate.

A problem is *not* network related when one or more of the following conditions exist:

- The problem lies within an individual application.
- The problem can be duplicated on the device when it is removed from the network.
- The problem is caused by a hardware failure.
- The problem is caused by user error.

Step 2

Isolate the problem using a top-down approach.

In this step, you'll identify the location of the problem. The administrative tools discussed earlier in this chapter are very helpful during this step. In a single network, problem isolation might be as easy as comparing the network map to a device list. As your network grows, however, and more devices and applications are added, problem isolation becomes more difficult. And as the number of users increases, so does the chance for user errors. One of the first steps to take is to determine the scope of the problem. Is the problem isolated to a single computer or does the problem occur from other computers as well? Is just one network affected or are other networks also affected?

The *top-down* approach to troubleshooting provides a set of step-by-step tasks designed to isolate problems systematically. Using this model, you begin by looking at the internet level (if you have an internet), and then continue by examining progressively smaller groups of hardware.

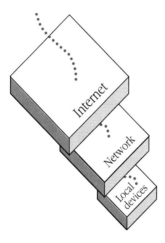

At the highest, or internet, level, you identify the networks affected by the problem. Is the problem isolated to a single network or are other networks involved? If more than one network is involved, are they connected? If all devices on a network are missing from a device list, the problem is likely to be router- or bridge-related. Make sure that routers and bridges have been properly configured. If you're using Ethernet or Token Ring, make sure that the hardware and software has been installed properly.

If no problems show up at the internet level, you then focus on the affected network to determine if problems exist. How many devices exhibit the problem? All of them? Some? Just one? Check to see if the amount of traffic is too heavy or if network specifications—such as cable length, the number of devices, or network topology—are being adhered to. Problems such as performance degradation and ghosting are often caused by exceeding network limitations.

At the lowest level, the local devices level, you isolate the specific device or devices involved. This might entail something as simple as generating a device list (through Inter•Poll, for example) and then comparing it to the network map, or it might involve something as detailed as checking each device for potential hardware and software problems (see the next step).

Step 3

Check and correct any hardware problems or software problems on localized devices.

Once you've isolated the problem to a specific network device, physically inspect the hardware to verify that all cables and connectors are intact and connected correctly. Also, verify that the device itself is functional. Intermittent problems on the network, such as the appearance and disappearance of a network device, can be caused by loose connections. Check cable extension connectors to make sure they are secure. If devices cannot communicate or performance becomes erratic, network breaks are usually at fault. Check for breaks at the connector, disconnected cable extenders, a severed cable, and broken or damaged connector pins.

If the hardware is not at fault, you are left with one more option—software. Check to see if the device is using a system file or a driver file (such as a LaserWriter driver) that is different from the version being used by other like devices.

Troubleshooting scenarios

The following scenarios illustrate the concepts presented in this chapter. Chris Regello—the network administrator—uses a systematic troubleshooting strategy and network tools such as Inter•Poll, the network map, and the Chooser to uncover and remedy the problems. As you work through these scenarios, refer to the network maps that accompany this section to see where the users and devices are located.

First Floor

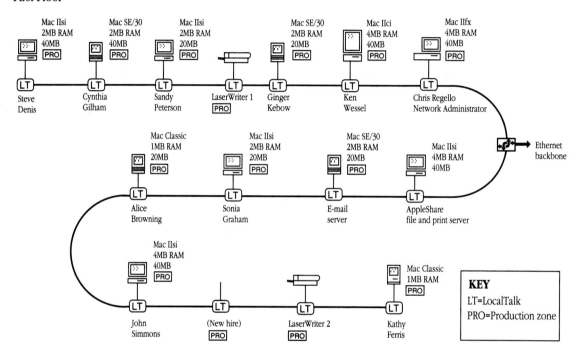

Second Floor

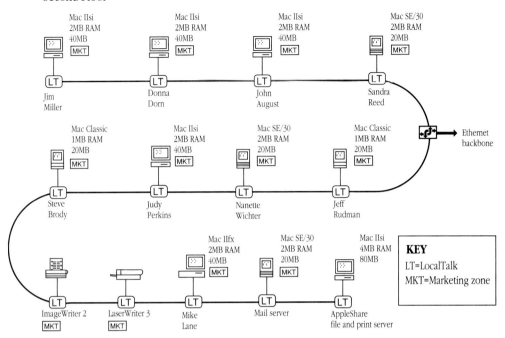

KEY
LT=LocalTalk
MKT=Marketing zone

Third Floor

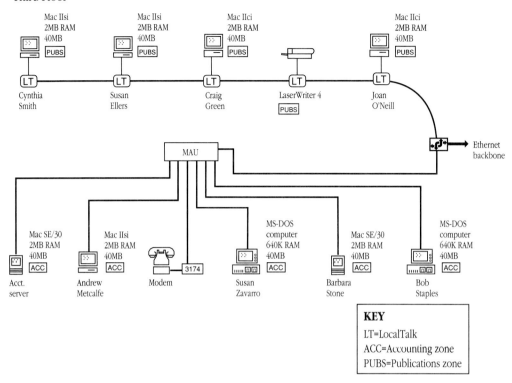

When Chris returns from lunch, she has two messages on her answering machine, from Cynthia Gilham and Ken Wessel, about E-mail problems.

Step 1

Define the symptoms of the problem and verify that the problem is network related.

Chris calls Cynthia for more information. Cynthia tells Chris that whenever she tries to send E-mail, she receives an error message. Chris then calls Ken. She learns that he's been printing and using the file server all morning, but he can't send E-mail to Cynthia. Chris checks with Steve and Sandy—the users on either side of Cynthia—to see if they are having problems. She learns that they have both been using the printer and sending E-mail messages all morning. Chris suspects that the problem is not network related.

Step 2

Isolate the problem using a top-down approach.

Because Cynthia seems to be the only user having problems, Chris believes that the problem is specific to Cynthia's computer. An Inter•Poll device list confirms Chris's suspicion: Cynthia's computer is the only device on the network missing from the list.

Step 3

Check and correct any hardware or software problems on the localized device.

Chris stops by Cynthia's office to check for problems. She opens the Chooser on Cynthia's computer and finds that no devices are displayed. Chris also quickly discovers the source of the problem—AppleTalk has been turned off in the Chooser, disabling the network connection.

Chris receives a call from two users complaining about network problems. John Simmons keeps receiving time-out errors on the LaserWriter when he tries to print mail. Alice Browning's Macintosh computer keeps telling her that it can't locate the LaserWriter when she tries to print.

Step 1

Define the symptoms of the problem and verify that the problem is network related.

Chris calls John and Alice. They tell her that they haven't been able to print to LaserWriter 2 all morning. Chris asks Alice if she's had any other problems. Alice tells her that she's sent and received E-mail that morning. Because the problem here involves devices that can't communicate, the problem is network related and seems to be a printing problem.

Step 2

Isolate the problem using a top-down approach.

Chris refers to the network map to get a clear picture of where LaserWriter 2 is in relation to John and Alice. She then generates a device list by running Inter•Poll. This list shows that LaserWriter 2 is not displayed. Because Alice has been able to use E-mail, Chris believes that the problem is specific to the printer.

Step 3

Check and correct any hardware or software problems on the localized device.

When Chris physically examines LaserWriter 2, she uncovers the source of the problem: the LocalTalk cable for the printer is not long enough and the strain has caused the cable to become partially unplugged. Chris adds another length of LocalTalk cable and a cable extender to remedy the problem.

John Simmons and Barbara Stone each tape messages to Chris's computer. John can't send E-mail to a coworker, Bob Staples, even though Bob is at his computer. Barbara receives an error message any time she tries to send E-mail to anyone.

Step 1

Define the symptoms of the problem and verify that the problem is network related.

Chris calls John, Barbara, and Bob to gather more information. John tells Chris that although he can't send E-mail to Bob, he has been able to send E-mail to Sonia. When Chris talks to Bob, he says that he can't access the printer. Barbara tells Chris that she's been having E-mail problems all afternoon, although this morning everything was fine. Using the remote-administration software on her computer, Chris watches while they reproduce the steps they took and confirms that there is, indeed, a problem. Because the symptoms involve more than one device and a clear inability to access network services, the problem is definitely network related.

Step 2

Isolate the problem using a top-down approach.

Chris checks the network map to locate John, Barbara, Bob and Sonia. John and Sonia are located on the first floor in the Production zone. Both Bob and Barbara are in the Accounting zone on the third floor. Chris calls Donna and Nanette on the second floor to see if they have had any problems and learns that all is fine. Chris generates a zone listing with Inter•Poll and sees that the Accounting zone is missing from this list.

Step 3

Check and correct any hardware or software problems on the localized device.

Because the Accounting zone is on a Token Ring network, Chris decides to check the multistation access unit (MAU) that connects all users on this network. Physical inspection fails to show a problem, but Chris replaces the MAU with a spare to see what happens. After she does this, she checks with the users in the Accounting group and finds that everything is fine again, indicating that the original MAU had been internally damaged.

Sonia Graham and Ginger Kebow are having network problems. Sonia can't access the printer she normally uses. Ginger can't send any E-mail.

Step 1

Define the symptoms of the problem and verify that the problem is network related.

Chris stops by to talk to Sonia and Ginger. Sonia tells her that she hasn't been able to use LaserWriter 1 to print the E-mail message she received from Kathy. Chris opens Sonia's Chooser window and sees that LaserWriter 1 is missing from the list of available printers. Chris then talks to Ginger. Ginger says that she's been printing to LaserWriter 1 all morning, but she can't send any E-mail. Chris realizes that this is a network problem, since more than one user is having trouble communicating with network devices.

Step 2

Isolate the problem using a top-down approach.

Chris studies the network map and focuses on the affected network to see where all devices and users are located. Since Sonia received mail from Kathy, Chris knows that the E-mail server is probably OK. And since Ginger has been able to use LaserWriter 1, the problem doesn't seem to be the printer. Since Chris is on the same network, she checks in her Chooser to see what's up. She can see the E-mail server, but can't see LaserWriter 1. Chris decides to check for a network break between her office and Ken's office.

Step 3

Check and correct any hardware or software problems on the localized device.

Chris examines the length of cable between her office and Ken's office and finds that everything is fine. She then checks Ken's office and discovers the problem: Ken took his computer home that morning and improperly disconnected it from the network. Instead of leaving the LocalTalk connector box in place and disconnecting the cable from the back of his computer, he took the connector box with him, causing a break in the network. Chris gets another connector box, reconnecting both sides of the network.

When Chris gets back from vacation, she has several notes taped to her computer—from Mike Lane, Judy Perkins, and Nanette Wichter—all complaining about network problems.

Step 1

Define the symptoms of the problem and verify that the problem is network related.

Chris first calls Mike, who subbed for her while she was gone. He tells her that, although he hasn't experienced any problems, he's had complaints from several users about all kinds of problems—printing, E-mail, and file service. Chris then talks to Judy, who complains that the network is "acting weird." When Chris asks her what she means, she says that she's had erratic response from the file server and printing is sometimes slow. When Chris calls Nanette, she tells Chris that she sometimes gets an error message when she tries to print. Because there is a clear problem in accessing network services, Chris concludes that the problem *is* network related.

Step 2

Isolate the problem using a top-down approach.

Chris checks the network map and sees that Mike, Judy, and Nanette are located in the Marketing zone on the second floor. Chris suspects that the problem is ghosting, since network services seem to be intermittent. Running Inter•Poll at different times supports her theory. Sometimes all the nodes in the Marketing zone are displayed, sometimes they are not. Since Mike is not experiencing any problems, but Judy and Nanette are, it looks like the problem is located between Judy and Mike. Chris decides to check the cable in this area.

Step 3

Check and correct any hardware or software problems on the localized device.

Chris carefully checks the cable between Judy's office and Mike's office and discovers a crimped section by the ImageWriter printer, probably caused by the recent moving activity. Chris replaces the cable in this section.

Chris has received a complaint from Steve Brody about slow printing.

Step 1

Define the symptoms of the problem and verify that the problem is network related.

Chris talks to Steve to find out more details. He tells her that he's been printing a lot of documents and it's been taking "forever." When she asks when the problem began, he said he didn't notice it until he started doing a lot of printing that day. Since this seems to be a problem with slow network service, Chris concludes that it is a network problem.

Step 2

Isolate the problem using a top-down approach.

Chris checks the network map to see where Steve sits: on the second floor in the Marketing zone. Since print delays can signal network degradation, Chris checks the traffic across the router to see if it shows excessive activity. The router statistics appear fine, so she then checks the traffic on Steve's network. Again, traffic appears normal. Chris then proceeds to a localized device check. Using Inter•Poll, she runs a device list to confirm that all network devices appear on this list. Finally, using Inter•Poll, she checks the system versions of the computers on Steve's network and discovers the problem: Steve's computer has an old printer driver. Talking to Steve again, she discovers that Steve had copied a game to his computer last week and while doing so, had inadvertently replaced his printer driver with an older version on the game disk. The printing delay was caused when he was printing multiple documents, causing the LaserWriter to reinitialize each time it accessed the old printer driver.

Step 3

Check and correct any hardware or software problems on the localized device.

Since Chris already pinpointed the exact problem during step 2, she simply replaces Steve's printer driver with the standard one being used on the rest of the network.

Susan Ellers calls Chris and says that she can't access the file server on the second floor.

Step 1

Define the symptoms of the problem and verify that the problem is network related.

Using remote-administration software, Chris watches while Susan attempts, unsuccessfully, to access the AppleShare file server on the second floor. Susan is following the correct steps, so it's not a matter of user error. Susan says that she has been printing to LaserWriter 4 all day and sending E-mail to Andrew Metcalfe, so the problem does seem to be network related: a problem communicating with the second floor file server.

Step 2

Isolate the problem using a top-down approach.

Chris looks at the network map of the building to get a sense of the big picture. Susan is located on the third floor of the building and the file server is on the second floor. There is a router and an Ethernet backbone linking the second and third floors. Chris begins to isolate the problem by looking at the internet level. Are any other networks affected by the problem? Since Chris is on the first floor, she tries to access the second floor file server to see what happens: she has no problems logging on. Chris begins to suspect a problem with the router between the second and third floors or a break in the Ethernet backbone cable. She continues to isolate the problem by starting with the easier possibility—a router problem. Chris runs an Inter•Poll device list and discovers that the router is, indeed, missing from this list.

Step 3

Check and correct any hardware or software problems on the localized device.

Chris goes up to the second floor to inspect the router and discovers an obvious problem: the router is turned off, severing the connection between the second and third floors.

Getting additional help

There may be times when you just can't find the solution to a network problem and you need to turn elsewhere for the answer. If you're the administrator of a network in a larger internet, there are probably more experienced administrators or in-house experts that you can consult. In-house support staff are intimately familiar with the details of your organization's networks. They also have access to the wide range of support services available from Apple and other providers.

There are also many other resources you can turn to, including:

- *Documentation and other references.* Sometimes, the answer you need is right at your fingertips—in the product manual. In addition, industry journals are an excellent source of up-to-date network tips. Relevant Apple manuals, computer journals, and other reference materials are listed in the Appendix.

- *Authorized Apple resellers.* In many cases, Apple resellers (including authorized Apple dealers) are your best source for answers. All Apple resellers provide both before- and after-sales support for Apple hardware and software. Apple supplies its resellers with the tools and information they need to provide this assistance, including training, reference materials, state-of-the-art diagnostic tools, timely spare parts delivery, and technical information. To locate your nearest authorized Apple reseller, call 1-800-538-9696.

- *Apple support representatives.* These are available directly through your company or through an authorized Apple dealership.

- *Consultants.* Qualified consultants are available to offer almost any kind of assistance, including integrated network support. The Apple Consultant Relations program provides participating consultants with regular mailings and other information to keep them up-to-date on the latest developments.

- *Electronic communication.* There are a variety of electronic mail services and electronic bulletin boards that provide an ideal way to exchange information about network-related problems and solutions. For more information, refer to the Appendix.

- *Apple User Groups.* User groups also provide a variety of support and training services, and are discussed in more detail in the Appendix.

- *Product vendors.* Your questions may be best answered by the maker or distributor of the network product you're using. Vendors usually include their phone numbers in their manuals, so you can call for more information about support options.

- *The Apple Customer Assistance Center.* If you've exhausted all other support channels, you can call the Apple Customer Assistance Center at 1-800-776-2333. This center is not a technical support line. It is designed to assist you with problems that, for whatever reason, are not resolved by your authorized Apple reseller.

Before you escalate a problem to an in-house expert or support representative, make sure you can duplicate the problem and that it's not a case of user error. Also, document the problem in detail. Think about what you would want to know if your network users came to you with a problem. Be sure to document when the problem occurs, how often it occurs, on which devices it occurs, and what applications are running when it occurs (including version numbers).

When you do receive help from an in-house expert or support representative, observe the procedure this person follows to solve the problem and document these procedures for future reference. If the problem is not immediately solved, you may need to continue documenting the problem over a period of time; resolution of some network problems requires experimentation and a detailed problem history.

Conclusion

Troubleshooting is a learned skill that combines experience, technical knowledge, a thorough understanding of your network, and some basic common sense. Using the three-step strategy and tools discussed in this chapter, you'll be well on your way to solving most network problems. As you discover helpful contacts and materials, keep notes and lists so you can build a ready source of backup for problems you can't solve alone. For specific information on trade journals, electronic communication, Apple User Groups, Apple product documentation, relevant reference materials, and other sources of additional support, turn to the Appendix.

Appendix: For More Information

This appendix points you to additional sources of information on the AppleTalk network system, Apple networking products and topics, and local area networks. Areas of discussion include trade journals, Apple User Groups, electronic communication, Apple product documentation, and reference books.

Trade journals on networking

You can find a wide assortment of computer journals at your local newsstand, bookstore, or library. Journals are an excellent source of the most up-to-date networking information, providing product reviews and comparisons, how-to tips, solutions to common problems, lists of user groups and bulletin board services, and news on the latest product and technology breakthroughs. New journals enter the industry continually, so shop around to see what's available. Some of the most popular journals are listed below.

- *Byte Magazine*
- *Communications Week*
- *Computer Currents*
- *Computer Weekly*
- *ComputerWorld*
- *Data Communications*
- *InfoWorld*
- *LAN Magazine*
- *LAN Technology*
- *LAN TIMES*
- *MacUser*
- *MacWeek*
- *MacWorld*
- *Management Information Systems Week*
- *MicroTimes*
- *Network World*
- *PC Week*
- *PC World*
- *The Macintosh Buyer's Guide*

Apple User Groups

Apple User Groups provide an open and dynamic forum for exchanging questions, answers, and ideas on a wide variety of topics. Most user groups publish newsletters and hold regular meetings to share information. User groups support special-interest groups, conduct seminars, maintain on-line bulletin board services to answer members' questions and keep them apprised of the latest Apple-oriented news, and often maintain demonstration and public-domain (noncopyrighted) software libraries. Many user groups have formed within corporations, government agencies, and universities. These groups usually cater to the specific work-related needs and interests of members.

For information about the Apple User Groups nearest you or about how to start a new group, call 1-800-538-9696, extension 500. Or write to:

The Apple User Group Connection
Apple Computer, Inc.
20525 Mariani Avenue, M/S 36AA
Cupertino, CA 95014-6299

Electronic communication

Exchanging electronic messages with other network administrators and Macintosh users can be an ideal way to solve problems and learn about a variety of networking topics. BMUG, AppleLink®, CompuServe, and BITNET are some commonly-used means of electronic communication; however, there are hundreds of special-interest bulletin board services throughout the country. Computer journals are a good source of information about specific bulletin boards and E-mail exchanges.

BMUG

BMUG—the Berkeley Macintosh Users Group—is the largest Macintosh user group in the country, with 8,000 members nationwide. BMUG bulletin boards are an excellent source of information on Macintosh issues. The bulletin board MACNET.ADMIN is devoted exclusively to issues germane to network administrators. You can contact BMUG at 415-549-BMUG.

AppleLink

AppleLink is an electronic mail and bulletin board service sponsored by Apple Computer. It provides a broad spectrum of information about Apple products, including information on new products, product updates, technical issues, training courses, and prices. Contact your Apple sales representative for information on getting an AppleLink account.

CompuServe

CompuServe is a comprehensive electronic on-line service that can provide you with a variety of technical information on computer-related topics. You can subscribe to Macintosh forums, which include MAUG—the Micro Networked Apple Users Group—by calling CompuServe at 1-800-848-8199.

BITNET

Individuals at universities and research centers in the U.S. use BITNET for electronic mail, information retrieval, and connection to other networks, in the U.S. and abroad. BITNET is sponsored by EDUCOM, a national organization for members of the academic community concerned with the role of computing and technology in higher education. One of the discussion groups on BITNET is Info-Mac Digest, which is an electronic forum on Macintosh-related topics. To find out more about BITNET, contact EDUCOM at 202-872-4200.

APDA (Apple Programmer's and Developer's Association)

APDA® provides a wide range of development products and documentation for programmers and developers who work on Apple equipment. Although APDA is primarily focused on developer-related services and material, it does provide some information that can be useful to network administrators, such as the following:

- *A Guide to Apple Networking and Communications Products* provides an overview of Apple Computer's networking and communications products for multivendor environments. It is intended primarily for those who make purchasing decisions about technical products, but is useful to anyone who wants more information on these products.

You can contact APDA at the following address and telephone number:

APDA
Apple Computer, Inc.
20525 Mariani Avenue, M/S 33G
Cupertino, California 95014-6299
1-800-282-APDA

The Apple Communications Library

The Apple Communications Library (ACL) is a series of technical books written and produced by Apple Computer, published by Addison-Wesley. This series provides complete information on Apple Computer's approach to networking and communications, and offers comprehensive material on a wide variety of topics for a vast range of readers—from basic-level users to network administrators and developers. This book—*Planning and Managing AppleTalk Networks*—is part of the ACL. Other titles in the ACL include:

- *AppleTalk Network System Overview,* a description of the AppleTalk network system and a variety of Apple networking products; primarily for developers and information decision makers.

- *Inside AppleTalk,* second edition, the definitive technical guide to the protocol architecture of the AppleTalk network system; for developers.

- *Inside the Macintosh Communications Toolbox,* the definitive reference volume for the Macintosh Communications Toolbox, Apple's strategic communications development platform and an integral part of system software version 7.0; for developers.

- *Understanding Computer Networks,* an introduction to networking and communications concepts and technologies; for readers with little or no familiarity with computer networks.

You can obtain these books at your local bookstore and from APDA (listed on the previous page). For large volume purchases, contact Addison-Wesley directly at 617-944-3700.

Apple product documentation

The following manuals are packaged with the associated Apple product. The products should be available at an authorized Apple dealer.

- *A/UX Network System Administration* provides information about connecting a Macintosh computer running A/UX to a variety of networks.

- *A/UX Networking Essentials* describes how you can use your Macintosh computer running A/UX to access files and resources on other networked computers.

- *Apple Ethernet AUI Adapter User's Guide* provides information about connecting a Macintosh computer to an Ethernet cable system that requires an AUI connection (such as fiber-optic cable).

- *Apple Ethernet Thin Coax Transceiver User's Guide* provides information about connecting a Macintosh computer to an Ethernet network using thin coaxial cable.

- *Apple Ethernet Twisted-Pair Transceiver User's Guide* provides information on connecting a Macintosh computer to an Ethernet network using twisted-pair cable.

- *Apple Ethernet LC Card User's Guide* provides instructions for installing an Ethernet LC Card in a Macintosh LC computer.

- *Apple Ethernet NB Card User's Guide* provides instructions for installing an Ethernet NB Card in a Macintosh computer.

- *Apple II Workstation Card User's Guide* is for Apple IIe users. It provides instructions on installing the workstation card to access an AppleTalk network and on using an AppleShare file server from an Apple IIe workstation.

- *Apple Inter•Poll Network Administrator's Guide* is for network administrators. It describes how to use the Inter•Poll network administrator's utility to maintain and troubleshoot an AppleTalk network.

- *Apple MacTCP Administrator's Guide* provides instructions for installing and configuring an implementation of the Transmission Control Protocol/Internet Protocol (TCP/IP) suite.

- *Apple TokenTalk NB User's Guide* provides installation and operation guidelines for those using Token Ring in their AppleTalk networks.

- *AppleShare File Server Administrator's Guide* is written for AppleShare network administrators. It describes the AppleShare file server, shows how to set up the server and workstations, discusses network startup, and summarizes maintenance and troubleshooting procedures.

- *AppleShare File Server Administrator's Supplement for Apple II Workstations* is a supplement to the *AppleShare File Server Administrator's Guide.* It explains the special steps needed to set up a file server so that it can be used by network users who have Apple IIGS or enhanced Apple IIe workstations.

- *AppleShare File Server User's Guide* is written for Macintosh users who want to learn how to use an AppleShare file server or print server. It describes the AppleShare file server, shows how to set up the workstation, tells how to access and use the file server, and summarizes troubleshooting procedures.

- *AppleShare PC User's Guide* is written for MS-DOS users who want to learn how to use an AppleShare file server.

- *AppleShare Print Server Administrator's Guide* explains how to set up a Macintosh computer as an AppleShare print server, describes how to use AppleShare to manage printing, and provides troubleshooting guidelines for the print server. This document also explains how to install the AppleShare workstation print software and access a print server from a workstation.

- *AppleTalk Internet Router Administrator's Guide* provides installation and operation guidelines for those using the AppleTalk Internet Router.

- *AppleTalk Network User's Guide for the Apple IIGS* explains how to set up and use Apple IIGS computers with an AppleShare file server.

- *AppleTalk Phase 2 Introduction and Upgrade Guide* describes the extensions to the AppleTalk network system provided by AppleTalk Phase 2 and also discusses the process of upgrading an internet to AppleTalk Phase 2.

- *Aristotle Administrator's Guide* describes how to use Aristotle, the menu-management program that provides users of Apple II computers with a streamlined method for starting up ProDOS® applications from an AppleShare file server.

- *LocalTalk Cable System Owner's Guide* is a brief reference guide to LocalTalk cable, hardware, and installation. Use it to help in the initial setup of your network and as a basic introduction to LocalTalk networks.

- *PATHWORKS for Macintosh* documentation, available through Digital Equipment Corporation, provides information on PATHWORKS for Macintosh software. The software includes VMS server software, Macintosh client applications, Macintosh-to-VAX network connectivity software, and developer tools.

- *System 7 Group Upgrade Guide* is a guide to upgrading multiple Macintosh computers to System 7.

Other Apple documents

Contact your regional Apple sales office or an authorized Apple dealer for information on the availability of the following publications.

- *Apple Multivendor Network Solutions Guide* provides information on integrating Macintosh computers into a multitude of computer environments, including network environments such as Novell and 3COM, MS-DOS-related environments, IBM host environments, Digital environments, and UNIX environments.

- *Creating and Managing an Academic Computer Lab* focuses on the specific issues pertinent to planning and managing a computer lab in the higher education classroom.

- *Introduction to the Apple-Digital Network Environment* provides information on the integrated Macintosh-to-VAX network environment and the associated support and services. Published jointly by Apple Computer and Digital Equipment Corporation.

- *Local Area Network Cabling Guide* provides you with an introduction to different types of LAN technologies and helps you choose the Apple network products that best fit your networking needs.

- *The Advantages of AppleTalk Phase 2* is for network administrators and describes the important advantages of Phase 2 and how it differs from Phase 1. It also includes upgrade information for people wanting to upgrade a Phase 1 internet to Phase 2.

Books about Macintosh networking

Look for the following books at your local computer bookstore or library.

Hands-On AppleTalk, by Mike Rogers and Virginia Bare. Published by Simon and Schuster. New York, New York. 1989.

IBM PC and Macintosh Networking, by Stephen L. Michel. Published by Hayden Books. Indianapolis, Indiana. 1988.

MacLANS: Local Area Networking With the Macintosh, by Mark D. Veljkov. Published by Scott, Foresman and Company. Glenview, Illinois. 1988.

The MS-DOS–Mac Connection, by Cynthia W. Harriman. Published by Simon and Schuster. New York, New York. 1988.

The Well-Connected Macintosh, by Tony Bove and Cheryl Rhodes. Published by Harcourt Brace Jovanovich. Orlando, Florida. 1987.

General networking books

The following books provide general reference information on local area networks. They should be available at your local computer bookstore or library.

A Manager's Guide to Local Networks, by Frank Defler and William Stallings. Published by Prentice-Hall, Inc. Englewood Cliffs, New Jersey. 1983.

Computer Networks, by Andrew S. Tanenbaum. Published by Prentice-Hall, Inc. Englewood Cliffs, New Jersey. 1981.

Introduction to Local Area Networks. Published by Digital Equipment Corporation. 1982.

Local Area Networking With Microcomputers: A Guide for the Business Decision-Maker, by Stevanne Ruth Lehrman. Published by Prentice Hall Press. New York, New York. 1986.

Local Area Networks in Large Organizations: A Manager's Briefing, by Thomas Wm. Madron. Published by Hayden Book Company. Hasbrouck Heights, New Jersey. 1984.

Local Area Networks: A User's Guide for Business Professionals, by James Harry Green. Published by Scott, Foresman and Company. Glenview, Illinois. 1985.

Local Area Networks: An Introduction to the Technology, by John E. McNamara. Published by Digital Press. Burlington, Massachusetts. 1985.

Networking: The Competitive Edge. Published by Digital Equipment Corporation. 1985.

Networking and Data Communication, by Victoria C. Marney-Petix. Published by Reston Publishing Company (a Prentice-Hall company). Reston, Virginia. 1986.

Understanding Computer Networks, by Apple Computer. Published by Addison-Wesley. 1989.

Glossary

active star A type of star topology in which a central controller sends transmissions to each device on the network. See also **star.**

addressing A scheme, determined by network protocols, for identifying the sending device and receiving device for any given item of information traveling on a network.

AFP See **AppleTalk Filing Protocol.**

Apple Ethernet Cable System A family of products from Apple Computer that provides connectivity to Ethernet networks. Includes media adapters for thin coax, twisted-pair, and other media. Also includes self-terminating thin coax cables. All Apple Ethernet products conform to the IEEE 802.3 standard for Ethernet.

Apple File Exchange An application that provides file transfer capability between the Macintosh file system and MS-DOS format.

AppleShare File Server A combination of AppleShare File Server software, one or more attached hard disks or CD-ROMs, and a Macintosh computer that allows users to store and share documents, folders, and applications over an AppleTalk network.

AppleShare Print Server A Macintosh computer, running AppleShare Print Server software, that stores documents sent to it over an AppleTalk network and manages the printing of the documents on a printer.

AppleTalk Filing Protocol The presentation-layer protocol that allows users to share data files and application programs that reside on a file server.

AppleTalk Internet Router A Macintosh computer running AppleTalk Internet Router software that connects up to eight AppleTalk networks. See also **router.**

AppleTalk Phase 2 An enhancement of the original AppleTalk network system. AppleTalk Phase 2 was introduced in June, 1989. Phase 2 enables users to build networks with thousands of AppleTalk devices, supports industry standards such as the Token Ring environment, and provides more efficient routing techniques to improve performance in large networks.

architectural map A type of network map that shows the network's structural elements, such as stairways, walls, and windows. Compare with **schematic map** and **skeleton map.**

archive backup Backup copies of a network's data stored for historical purposes.

backbone network A central network that connects a number of other, usually lower-speed networks. The backbone network is typically constructed with a high-speed communication medium.

backbone router   A router that is used to connect networks through a backbone network so that networks can be linked in a nonserial manner.

background printing   A software application that runs on a computer as a background process, allowing the user to work on other tasks while a document is being printed. Background printing may occasionally slow the computer's performance until the document is actually sent to the printer. See also **background process.** Compare with **print server.**

background process   A procedure that runs while the user is using another application. See also **MultiFinder.**

bandwidth   The range of transmission frequencies that a network can use. The greater the bandwidth, the greater the amount of information that can travel on the network at one time.

bridge   A device that connects two networks of the same type together (such as two Ethernet networks). The connected networks form a single large network. Compare with **router.**

broadcast traffic   A network transmission technique in which packets are sent to all nodes on a network simultaneously.

bus   A network layout that uses a single cable to connect all the devices in a sequential line. Messages are broadcast along the whole bus, and each network device listens for and receives messages directed to its unique address.

callback   A security precaution in which a user's preauthorized phone number is verified before allowing the user to connect to a network from a remote location.

carrier sensing   A technique that allows multiple devices on a bus network to gain access to a shared transmission medium. Each device listens until no signals are detected, and then begins transmitting. Transmissions are sent to all connected devices. To receive a transmission, a device must recognize its own address.

CD-ROM   Abbreviation for Compact Disc Read-Only Memory. A compact disc can store large amounts of information.

ceiling grid system   A cable distribution system running through a ceiling that is composed of prefabricated ducts.

cellular floors   A cable distribution system consisting of trenches and distribution cells that are built into the floor.

centralized file service   File service that is provided by a central server accessed by network users. Compare with **distributed file sharing.**

Chooser   A desk accessory that lets a network user select shared devices, such as printers and file servers.

clear text   Data that is sent on the network in unencrypted form.

client computer   A computer on a network that receives network services from a server.

closed shaft system   An enclosed area in which cables rise in a direct vertical line between floors.

coaxial cable   An electrical cable consisting of a central wire surrounded by a second tubular wire made of braided mesh, both of which have the same center point, or axis, hence the name *coaxial.* Separated from the central wire by insulation, the tubular wire shields electronic impulses traveling along the central wire. In turn, the tubular wire is surrounded by insulation.

components   The functional elements that can be used on a network, such as computing and peripheral devices, connection hardware, and software.

computer virus   A computer program, added to otherwise harmless software, that can cause a variety of problems. A virus can infect a system without causing great harm—by displaying a message, for example—or it can do great damage—such as erasing a hard disk.

conduit   Metal or plastic tubing used to protect and insulate electrical wiring. Often required by building codes.

constant voltage transformer (CVT) A device that supplies constant voltage regardless of variations in the electricity supply.

data lockout program A program installed on a computer that is used to protect files by providing password protection.

dial-in service A network service that enables users to access network resources, such as printers and file servers, from a remote location (via a modem).

direct delivery A type of electronic mail system in which messages are sent directly from one computer to another. Compare with **mail server.**

distributed file sharing A type of file service in which users can share the contents of their hard disks with other users on the network. Compare with **centralized file service.**

driver A program that controls the operations of a peripheral device, such as a printer or modem.

drop A means by which devices are connected to a cable on a bus network.

drop folder A folder that serves as a private mailbox for individuals. Once someone places a file in a drop folder, only the owner of the drop folder can retrieve it. Users can create drop folders by setting the appropriate AppleShare or Macintosh file sharing access privileges.

dynamic node ID assignment The AppleTalk addressing scheme that assigns node IDs dynamically, rather than associating a permanent address with each node. Dynamic node ID assignment facilitates adding and removing nodes from the network by preventing conflicts between old node IDs and new node IDs.

earth ground An object that makes an electrical connection with the earth.

electromagnetic interference Interference that can affect the reliable transmission of network data. Sources include radio transmitters, fluorescent lights, elevators, and industrial machinery.

electronic mailbox An area on a mail server that stores a user's messages until they are requested by the user.

E-mail Stands for electronic mail. A network service that allows users to send messages and files to each other. E-mail often includes abilities to send, receive, sort, and save messages.

encrypt A way to protect data by coding it so that it appears to be a random sequence of characters. Only those with the password can unscramble the data.

Ethernet A 10 megabits-per-second (Mbps) network standard originally developed by Digital Equipment Corporation, Intel Corporation, and Xerox Corporation. Ethernet was standardized by the IEEE 802.3 committee.

EtherTalk Software that enables AppleTalk protocols to run over industry-standard Ethernet technology.

fiber-optic cable A transmission medium that uses light to send a signal.

file-by-file backup A method for backing up data that creates copies of individual files, one at a time. Compare with **volume backup.**

file server Hardware and/or software that allows users to store and share documents, folders, and applications over a network.

file server attributes Characteristics associated with file server folders, such as who owns the folder and what the access privileges to that folder are.

file server–aware Applications designed to be used on or with file servers. Applications that are file server–aware provide document management to ensure the integrity of data. Also referred to as *AppleShare-aware.*

file translator A utility program that converts a file from one computer format to another, such as from Macintosh to MS-DOS. Apple File Exchange is a file translator that is supplied with Macintosh system software.

gateway A combination of hardware and software that enables networks using different protocols to communicate with one another. For example, a gateway can connect an AppleTalk network with a network using non-AppleTalk protocols, such as TCP/IP.

ghosting A term used to describe the intermittent appearance and disappearance of network devices.

group A named collection of one or more registered file server users. Groups are created for users who usually have common interests and share information.

guest A user who is logged on to an AppleShare file server without a registered user name and password. A guest cannot own a directory or folder.

half-bridge A device used to connect two remote networks over a telecommunications link.

half-router A router that is used to connect two or more remote networks over a telecommunications link. Each network is connected to a router, which in turn is connected to a modem. This combination of two half-routers serves, in effect, as a single routing unit. Also called a *remote router.*

hop A unit count between networks on an internet. Signifies "one router away."

IEEE See **Institute of Electrical and Electronic Engineers.**

incremental backup A type of file-by-file backup that saves only the data that has been created or changed since the last backup was done.

infrared light A means of transmitting network data without physical cables. It is basically the same technology used to send remote signals to a TV set.

INIT files Special application programs that customize your System file. In System 7, these are called *system extensions.*

Institute of Electrical and Electronic Engineers (IEEE) An association of engineering societies that develops industry standards. The IEEE 802 committee

defined many of the standards for today's local area networks.

internet Two or more networks connected by internet routers. Networks in an internet can share information and services. See also **router.**

Inter•Poll Software from Apple that helps administrators monitor the network and diagnose the source of problems that arise.

key A password used to encrypt and decrypt files.

launch To put a program into action; to start a program.

local router An internet router used to connect AppleTalk networks that are in close proximity to each other. The local router is directly connected to each of the AppleTalk networks that it links.

LocalTalk A type of AppleTalk network that is inexpensive and easy to set up. LocalTalk is commonly used to connect small- to medium-sized workgroups.

LocalTalk cable system Shielded twisted-pair cable from Apple that comes in preassembled kits and in custom wiring kits. A basic kit contains a prepared length of cable, a connector box, and a cable extender. The custom kit allows you to create custom-length cables.

logbook A historical record of network activity that is typically maintained by network administrators. Specialized logbooks can track backup activity, equipment and supplies, and network numbers and zone names.

loop A type of ring topology in which devices are connected in a closed circle, with each device wired directly to the next by means of the shortest physical path. A controller directs transmissions on the network. Compare with **star-wired ring** and **true ring.**

loopback test A network test that enables an administrator to send packets to a specific device to check for problems in the transmission path.

Macintosh File Sharing A built-in feature of System 7 that enables users to share the contents of their hard disks with other users on the network.

mail server A computer with one or more hard disks for storing electronic messages and files.

MAU See **multistation access unit.**

medium The means by which devices on a network are linked together to communicate and share information. Types of media include physical cables as well as infrared light.

modem A contraction of modulator-demodulator. A device that enables a computer or terminal to transmit over telephone lines by modulating, or converting, data from a digital to analog form. When originating a call, the modem modifies its analog carrier signal to carry a digital signal; when answering a call, the modem extracts the digital signal from the modified carrier.

modem server A combination of hardware and software that enables many people to share a single modem. See also **modem.**

MultiFinder In system software prior to version 7.0, a multitasking operating system for Macintosh computers that enables several applications to be open at the same time. In addition, processes (such as print spooling) can operate in the background so that users can perform one task while the computer performs another. In System 7, the multitasking capabilities of MultiFinder have been incorporated into the Finder.

multi-launch, multi-user application An application that allows more than one person to use a single copy of an application when it resides on a file server and that allows more than one person to open or change the same file at the same time.

multi-launch, single-user application An application that allows more than one person to open a single copy of an application when it resides on a file server, but that allows only one person at a time to open a particular file and change it.

multistation access unit (MAU) In a Token Ring network, a lobe concentrator that physically connects computers and other devices to the ring; a wiring concentrator. Relays in the MAU provide for physical insertion to, and detachment from, the ring.

Name Binding Protocol The AppleTalk transport-level protocol that translates a character string into a network address.

NBP See **Name Binding Protocol.**

network map A graphic representation of a network's physical layout.

network number A 16-bit number that provides a unique identifier for a network in an AppleTalk internet.

network performance A measure of how smoothly and responsively the network is operating. When network performance is adequate, users will receive network services without any noticeable delays. When performance is poor, bottlenecks occur and users will notice slowdowns in network services.

network range A unique range of contiguous network numbers that is used to identify each Ethernet and Token Ring network on an AppleTalk internet.

network services The capabilities that the network system delivers to users, such as printing on network printers, file sharing on network file servers, or communicating through electronic mail.

network type A term used to describe different types of networks, such as LocalTalk, Ethernet, and Token Ring.

network zone list The list of zone names associated with an Ethernet or Token Ring network.

node An individually addressable device connected to an AppleTalk network, such as a computer or a LaserWriter printer.

node ID See **node number.**

node number A unique number used to identify each node on a network.

open shafts   Areas where unenclosed cables pass from floor to floor.

open system architecture   A protocol architecture, such as the AppleTalk protocol architecture, which is openly published so that developers can implement the protocols on other computer platforms or can replace protocols at any layer with different ones.

Open Systems Interconnection (OSI) model   A reference model for describing network protocols, devised by the International Standards Organization (ISO). This model divides protocols into seven layers to standardize and simplify protocol definitions.

OSI Model   See **Open Systems Interconnection model.**

overhead traffic   Network activity that is generated by devices on the network. Examples of overhead traffic include routers updating routing tables and E-mail message alerts. Compare with **user-generated traffic.**

packet   One unit of information that has been formatted for transmission on an AppleTalk network. A packet includes user data as well as the control and addressing information needed to send the packet to the correct destination.

passive star   A type of star topology that has a fairly low limit on the number of branches allowed and the total length of the cable.

performance degradation   A term used to describe an abnormal delay in network operations.

plenum air return   An enclosed ceiling space that carries used room air. Such a space may also carry flames rapidly. In other ceiling designs, used room air is carried in air ducts, somewhat reducing the fire danger.

plenum cable   A fire-retardant cable that is commonly used in plenum air returns and in other areas with a high fire risk. LocalTalk Custom Cable and Apple Ethernet Self-Terminating Cable (13 meter) are examples of plenum cable coated with Teflon. See also **plenum air return.**

PostScript   Adobe's programming language designed for communication with image-oriented printers, such as Apple's LaserWriter printers.

PrintMonitor   A background print spooler that is included with the Macintosh MultiFinder.

print server   A combination of hardware and software that stores documents sent to it over a network and manages the printing of the documents on a printer. A print server completely frees a computer of a printing task so that the computer is free to be used for other work. Compare with **background printing.**

protocol analyzer   Specialized software or hardware that enables an administrator to examine individual packets in order to uncover problems on the network.

protocol architecture   The system of network protocols that determines how the network's components—such as devices, cable, and software—work together to provide network services to users.

protocols   A formal set of rules for sending and receiving information on a network.

punchdown block   A wiring distribution block that is usually located in a telephone wiring closet.

PVC cable   Cable housed in PVC (polyvinyl chloride). PVC cable may emit toxic fumes if burned and is intended for use in low fire hazard areas unless it is placed in conduit.

raceway   A channel or molding for holding electrical wiring. Surface raceways may be located along baseboards or around walls at desktop height. Metal raceways are recommended for LocalTalk cable.

raised floor   A floor that is built over existing flooring, and that is made of interlocking plates supported by metal standards. The area under the raised floor can be used to install cable.

redundant routing   A technique in which duplicate routes are created to each network in an internet.

remote administration   A means of performing administrative tasks from a remote location. Remote administration software allows an administrator to view and operate another computer on the network.

repeater   A device that amplifies an electrical signal received from one piece of transmission medium and passes it on to another, similar, piece of transmission medium. A repeater is commonly used to extend a cable beyond its recommended maximum length.

riser system   Vertical structures extending from floor to floor through which utility lines can pass.

rollover method   A method used to reduce the cost of media used for backup purposes. Backups are kept on disk or tape for a scheduled period of time and then the media is reused to back up new data.

router   A device that connects networks together, isolating traffic within each network. The networks can be of the same type (such as two LocalTalk networks) or of different types (such as LocalTalk and Ethernet). A router receives data transmitted from other networks and retransmits it to its proper destination over the most efficient route; this route may include several routers, each forwarding the data to the next. Compare with **bridge, gateway,** and **repeater.**

routing table   A table, resident in each AppleTalk internet router, that serves as a map of the internet, specifying the path and distance (in hops) between the internet router and other networks. Routing tables are used to determine whether and where a router will forward a data packet.

schematic map   A type of network map that details the network's arrangement of devices and cable schematically.

SCSI   Stands for *Small Computer System Interface*. An industry-standard interface that provides high-speed access to peripheral devices.

security   The process of protecting data from unauthorized access, alteration, or destruction.

server   A network device that provides a service to network users, such as shared access to a file system (a

file server), control of a printer (a printer server), or storage of messages in a mail system (a mail server).

shared printing   A way to set up shared printing in which users send their documents directly to a printer. Before users can go on to other tasks, they must wait for their documents and all documents ahead of theirs to finish printing. Compare with **background printing** and **print server.**

single-copy license   An agreement that requires you to purchase one copy of software for each computer on which you plan to use it.

single-launch, multi-user applications   Applications that allow just one person at a time to open an application, but that allow two or more people to open or change the same file at the same time.

single-launch, single-user applications   Applications in which only one person at a time can open the application and only one person at a time can open a file and change it.

site license   An agreement that allows you to buy one copy of software for a fixed number of computers. Site licenses are often purchased to authorize applications for use on file servers.

skeleton map   A type of network map that is used to visualize interconnected networks in an internet.

spooler   An application that stores users' documents so they can be sent to the printer for printing while the users continue to do other work. Spool stands for *simultaneous peripheral operations on line.*

star   A network layout in which cable and devices radiate from a central point.

star-wired ring   A ring network in which the cable between devices passes through a central wire center called a *multistation access unit*. See also **multistation access unit.** Compare with **true ring** and **loop.**

store-and-forward device   A device, such as a mail server, that stores messages from one computer and then forwards the message on to the destination computer when requested by the recipient.

taps   The means by which devices are connected along a length of cable on a bus network.

10BASE-T   An IEEE standard for unshielded twisted-pair Ethernet networks. Twisted-pair cable that meets the 10BASE-T standard is made up of two pairs of wires twisted around each other so that external interference is equal in each pair, minimizing its effect.

terminating resistor   An electronic device that provides a proper endpoint for a bus network. The Apple Ethernet Thin Coax Transceiver and Apple Ethernet cables have built-in terminating resistors. Also referred to as a *terminator.*

throughput   The amount of work performed by a computer or related device or the amount of data passed through a network over a period of time.

time-domain reflectometer   Sophisticated network troubleshooting equipment that can pinpoint the location of electrical shorts and breaks, locate cable in walls, and measure the exact length of cable segments.

token passing   A network access method in which devices on a network pass a special sequence of bits, known as the "token," from one device to the next. A device can only transmit data on the network if it is in possession of the token.

Token Ring   An industry standard network type that is commonly used to connect IBM mainframes and IBM PCs. Token Ring networks are arranged in a ring topology in which devices pass tokens from one attaching device to another.

TokenTalk   Software that enables AppleTalk protocols to run over industry-standard (IEEE 802.5) Token Ring networks.

topology   The physical layout of a network, including the cables and devices.

traffic   Transmissions traveling across a network. Traffic is generated whenever two devices on the network communicate.

transceiver   A computer's hardware mechanism through which network transmissions are sent and received. The term is a combination of the words transmitter and receiver.

transceiver cable   Cable that is "dropped" from the ceiling to the workspace, allowing devices to be connected to a cable on a bus network. Also called a *drop cable.*

transmission medium   See **medium.**

transparent   The quality of a network that enables people to use network-based resources in the same way that they use local resources. The AppleTalk network system allows users to access network resources by means of the standard Macintosh desktop interface.

true ring   A type of ring topology in which devices are connected in a closed circle, with each device wired directly to the next by means of the shortest physical path. Messages travel automatically from one device to the next. Compare with **loop** and **star-wired ring.**

twisted-pair cable   A low-cost cable type that consists of two wires that are individually insulated and then twisted together. Includes standard telephone wire as well as shielded twisted-pair cable, such as LocalTalk cable, which has extra shielding properties.

underfloor duct systems   A kind of cable distribution system that consists of prefabricated pipes installed into the floor to provide protection and transport for cables.

uninterruptible power supply (UPS)   Backup power for a computer system when the electrical power fails or drops to an unacceptable voltage level. Small UPS systems provide battery power for only a few minutes— enough to power down the computer in an orderly manner. Sophisticated systems are tied to electrical generators and can provide power for days.

user-generated traffic   Network activity that is generated by user requests and that constitutes the majority of network traffic. Examples include accessing the file server, using the Chooser, and printing documents. Compare with **overhead traffic.**

virus-checking station A non-networked computer equipped with virus-detection software that is used to scan diskettes for possible virus infection.

volume A file storage unit on a file server that can consist of a hard disk or a CD-ROM disc.

volume backup A type of network backup that creates an exact duplicate of all data; usually used to quickly back up an entire hard drive. Compare with **file-by-file backup.**

zone A logical grouping of devices in an AppleTalk internet that makes it easier for users to locate network services. The network administrator defines zones during the router setup process.

zone name A name defined for each zone in an AppleTalk internet. A LocalTalk network can have just one zone name. Ethernet and Token Ring networks can have multiple zone names, called a *zone list*. See also **zone and network zone list.**

Index

A

active star topology 74, 75, 253
activity on network. *See* traffic
adding network services 199
adding users 197–198
addressing 18–19, 253
    on bus 73
    dynamic node ID assignment 20
    Name Binding Protocol (NBP)
        and 21
    network ranges and 120
ADPA 247
AFP. *See* AppleTalk Filing Protocol (AFP)
alert messages 55
AlisaShare 49, 51
Apple Communications Library (ACL)
    248
Apple Consultant Relations
        program 240
Apple Customer Assistance Center 241
Apple Ethernet 223
    port 89
Apple Ethernet AUI Adapter 93
Apple Ethernet Cable System 89–93, 253
Apple Ethernet LC Card 87, 89
Apple Ethernet NB Card 87, 89

Apple Ethernet Thin Coax
        Transceiver 90–91
    terminators for 223
Apple Ethernet Twisted-Pair
        Transceiver 92
Apple File Exchange 52, 253
AppleLink 245, 246
Apple product documentation 249–251
Apple Programmer's and Developer's
        Association 247
Apple resellers and dealers 240
AppleShare file server 18, 40–46, 253
    access privileges for 45–46
    aware applications 205
    backups and 190
    configuration guidelines 106
    example of access privileges 44
    file security 44
    management features 46
    number of users on 103
    passwords 41, 42
    reports with 181
    user access 42–43
    version of 173
    volumes 40–41
AppleShare Print Server 35–36, 253
    reports with 181–182
Apple support representatives 240
AppleTalk file servers 37–40

AppleTalk Filing Protocol (AFP) 38, 253
    non-AppleShare file servers
        and 49–52
AppleTalk Internet Router 18, 253
    monitoring network traffic with 178
    running concurrently with file
        service 104
    troubleshooting and 218
AppleTalk Network System Overview 248
AppleTalk Personal Network
        connectors 223
AppleTalk Phase 2 253
    network ranges and 120
Apple II, AppleShare Print Server 35–36
Apple II Workstation Card 82
Apple IIe 15
    LocalTalk and 82
Apple IIGS 15
    LocalTalk and 82
Apple User Group Connection 245
Apple user groups 240, 245
application protocols 11, 14
architectural map 130–131, 253
archive backups 186, 253
ARCnet 95
AUI (Attachment Unit Interface)
        Adapter 93
A/UX operating system 15

B

backbone networks 82, 253
  Ethernet as 87–88
  function of 122–124
  ghosting and 224
  placing shared devices on 127
  routers connecting networks to 113, 114, 254
  selecting types of 124
backbone router 113, 114, 254
background printing 33, 253–254
  or print server 36
background process 33, 254
backing up 151
  archive backups 186, 253
  considerations for 186–187
  examples of schedules 188–189
  file server attributes 183
  file-by-file backup 184, 255
  incremental backup 184, 256
  media 185–186
  rollover method of 186, 259
  schedules for 186–189
  segmenting backups 186
  servers 190
  shared files 183–191
  types of 183–184
  user files on individual computers 191
  virus prevention and 162
  volume backup 183–184
Backup Log 169–170
balanced networks, creating 99–101
bandwidth 62, 254
  of coaxial cable 65
BITNET 245, 246
BMUG (Berkeley Macintosh Users Group) 245, 246
boldfaced terms 8
bottlenecks 208–212
bridges 16, 17, 18, 110, 254
  for exceeded cable length limitations 223
broadcast traffic 110, 254

building codes 136
bus topology 72–74, 254
  address recognition 73
  for Ethernet 87
  ghosting in 222
  for LocalTalk 82
  for LocalTalk cable system 83

C

cable extenders
  disconnected cable extenders 221
  loose extenders 223
cable layout
  ceiling systems 141–143
  floor cable layouts 143–164
  handling cable 139
  labeling cables 139
  in multiroom/multifloor site 140–146
  planning of 138–146
  in single room 140
  underfloor installations 143–146
cables. See also coaxial cable; fiber-optic cable; infrared light; twisted-pair cables
  budget for 63
  damaged or obstructed cables 221
  exceeded length limitations 223
  severed cable 221
  testers 218
calendars for group 18
callback procedure 56, 159, 254
carrier sensing 72, 74, 254
cc:Mail 55
CD-ROM 254
  AppleTalk file servers 37–40
ceiling grid system 142, 254
ceiling system cable layout 141–143, 254
cellular floors, laying cable in 145, 254
centralized file service 39–40, 254
  security for 157
Chooser 254
  for AppleShare file service 42
  ghosting 222

Macintosh File Sharing 48
  names and 21
  and non-AppleShare AFP file servers 49–50
  troubleshooting and 218
  zone names and 118
clear text passwords 180, 254
client computer 18, 254
closed air returns 141
closed shaft systems 143, 254
coaxial cable 16, 65–67, 254
coexistence 205
collision avoidance 74
collision detection 74
compatibility categories for file server 204–205
components 10, 15, 254
CompuServe 245, 246
computer viruses. See viruses
computing and peripheral devices 15–16
conduit 136, 138, 254
connecting different network types 107
connection devices 10, 108–121. See also backbone networks; bridges; gateways; repeaters; routers
  hardware 16–17
  OSI model and 111
  placement of 125–127
connection protocols 11, 14
connector pin damage 221
connectors
  break at 221
  loose connector contact 223
constant voltage transformer (CVT) 136, 254
consultants, use of 240
continuity checkers 218
  for damaged or obstructed cables 221
copyright issues 203, 207–208
CRC errors. See cyclic redundancy check errors
cryptanalysis 157

Intel-based computers 49
interception of network signals 159–163
interface cards 16
    for Ethernet 89
    for LocalTalk 82
    for Token Ring networks 94
intermittent loss of services or
        devices 222–224
International Standards Organization
        (ISO)
    layered network protocols reference
        model 12
    Open Systems Interconnection (OSI)
        model, 12, 13–14
internet 3, 256. *See also* routers; zones
    AppleTalk Internet Router 178
    defined 16
    network number or range 119–121
    redundant routing 116
    routing table and 112
    skeleton maps 132
    topologies combined in 77–78
    traffic crossing routers in 177
Inter•Poll 18, 256
    Administration disk 133
    damaged or obstructed cables 221
    device list 172–173, 229
    driver incompatibility and 225
    integrity of network and 174–176
    network reports with 180–182
    system version identification
        173–174, 225
    troubleshooting and 218
    upgrading system software and 196
    versions of software and
        173–174, 225

J
junction sites 144

K
key for encryption 156, 256
kinking in cable 139

L
labeling cables 139
LANSTAR 95
LaserWriter printers 31
    driver incompatibility 225
    for Ethernet networks 87
    identifying versions of driver 173
    LocalTalk and 82
    nodes and 18–19
launching applications 203, 205, 256
    determining characteristics of
        206–207
layered protocols, Open Systems
        Interconnection (OSI) model, 12,
        13–14
length errors 175
Liaison 56
licensing issues 18, 203, 207–208
linking networks 107
local building codes 136
local routers, 113, 114, 256
LocalTalk 22, 82–86, 256
    bus topology for 72
    cable installations 138
    carrier sensing with collision
        avoidance 74
    driver 17
    with Ethernet backbone 87–88
    exceeded cable length limitations
        223
    ImageWriter printers and 31
    improper terminators for 222
    with infrared connections 86
    network number 119–121
    performance of 102
    with PhoneNET cable system 85
    repeaters with 109
    star topology 74
    too many devices on 222–223
    traffic on 101
    transmission speed of 82
    type of computer to use as a
        server 103

with unshielded twisted-pair cables
        85
    zone names on 119
LocalTalk cable system 83-84, 222, 256
    expansion of 84
LocalTalk Custom Cable 136
LocalTalk Option Card 82
location of users 26
logbooks 168–171, 256
    Network Activity Log 168–169
    troubleshooting and 218
    types of 169–170
logging on to AppleShare file servers 42
loopback test, 174–176, 256
loop topology 76, 256
Lotus 1-2-3, file translators in 52

M
MacDraw II 133
Macintosh
    as an AppleShare File Server 40–46
    as an AppleShare Print Server 35–36
    BMUG 245, 246
    books on networking 252
    connecting to Ethernet 87
    connecting to Token Ring 94
    LocalTalk and 82
    routers on 112
Macintosh File Sharing 47–49, 256
    access to 48
    monitoring of 48
    turning on 47–48
    use of 48
MACLAN Connect 49
MACNET.ADMIN 245
macros using passwords 155
MacTCP 88
mail servers 54–55, 256
maintenance 6, 166
    of cable 63
    labeling cables for 139
    of multistation access unit (MAU) 77
    of star topology 75
    of star-wired ring topology 77